AF497753

Society Building and Social Governance in China

Shen Yang

CANUT INTERNATIONAL PUBLISHERS

Istanbul - Berlin - London - Santiago - Cape Town

Society Building and Social Governance in China

Author: Shen Yang

Translators: Zhao Zhiyun, Zheng Haicui, Shen Yang, Chen Tianxiao

Editor: Deniz Kizilcec

Original Title: 中国社会建设与治理 / Zhongguo Shehui Jianshe Yu Zhili

Copyright © Shen Yang, Beijing Times Chinese Press Co., Ltd., April 2020

Canut International Publishers

Canut Intl. Turkey, Batı Mh. Karanfil Sk. 10/5, Pendik, Istanbul, Turkey

Canut Intl. Germany, Yorckstr. 66, D-10969, Berlin, Germany

Canut Intl. United Kingdom, 12a Guernsay Road, London E11 4BJ, England

Copyright © Canut International Publishers, October 2021

ISBN: 978-605-4923-58-8

Also available as e-book

www.canutbooks.com

About the Author

Shen Yang, current Director of the Research Department of Theoretical System of Socialism with Chinese Characteristics in the Academy of Marxism attached to CASS, master supervisor and associate researcher. During 2005-2008, he studied in the Academy of Marxism attached to the CASS and received the Doctor of Law degree.

His research mainly focuses on Society building and social governance in China, socialism with Chinese characteristics, Party building, collective economy in rural areas. He wrote four monographs: *Society Building and Social Governance in China*; *Reform and Opening-up and Early Period Practice of the Socialism with Chinese Characteristics*; *Glorious Journey: Theory and Practice of Socialism with Chinese Characteristics*; *A Comparison on the Essence of Democratic Socialism with the Socialism with Chinese Characteristics*. More than 40 articles written by him were published in newspapers and academic journals.

His book *Glorious Journey: Theory and Practice of Socialism with Chinese Characteristics* won the Outstanding Book Award of the Chinese Academy of Social Sciences in 2016.

Address: No. 5 Jianguomen Nei Dajie, Academy of Marxism,
Chinese Academy of Social Sciences, Beijing 100732, P. R. China.
E-mail: sydwyyx@163.com
Mobile: 0086-18518257099
WeChat: 18518257099

Preface

Strengthening Society Building and Enhancing People's Welfare

On November 15, 2012, at a press conference with domestic and foreign reporters, Xi Jinping said in his speech: "Our people love life and expect better education, more stable jobs, better income, more reliable social security, medical care of a higher standard, more comfortable living conditions, and a more beautiful environment. They hope that their children can grow up better, work better and live better. People's yearning for a good and beautiful life is the goal for us to strive for."[1] Xi Jinping's words are simple, far-reaching, and serious, full of deep feelings for the people, and show Chinese communists' "people-centered" sentiments. In August 2013, Xi Jinping made a clear request at the National Propaganda and Ideology Work Conference: "We must establish a work orientation with the people at the center." "Putting the people at the center means that we must make realizing, safeguarding and developing the basic interests of the broadest people into our starting point and stopover point. This is the Party's fundamental mission of for whose sake, relying on whom."

"People's yearning for a good and beautiful life is the goal for us to strive for" – this sonorous, powerful and resounding proposition shows the Chinese communists' political stance of "putting the people at the center". The same proposition was repeatedly emphasized by Xi Jinping. In a joint interview with the media of BRICS countries, Xi Jinping pointed out: "The Communist Party of China in power should lead people to build a better country and make their lives better." In an exclusive interview with the

---

1 *A Series of Important Speeches by General Secretary Xi Jinping* (2016), compiled by the Publicity Department of the CPC Central Committee: Learning Press, People's Press, 2016, p. 212.

Russian TV, Xi Jinping again emphasized: "The Communist Party of China upholds utilizing power for the people and the people's yearning for a better life is our mission. My ruling philosophy, if summarized in a sentence, is to serve the people and shoulder my responsibilities." People's yearning for a good and beautiful life pointed out by Xi Jinping is precisely the basic orientation of society building and social governance towards which the the Communist Party of China is leading the Chinese people. Strengthening society building and social governance is the inevitable requirement of carrying out the five major development concepts of innovation, coordination, green, openness and sharing, and the historical necessity for the CPC to maintain close ties with the broad masses of the people and consolidate the ruling foundation and ruling position of the the Communist Party of China.

In recent years, the Chinese government has strengthened society building and social governance. Since the 18th CPC National Congress, with the constant improvement of the material and cultural living standards of the Chinese people, the people' demands for public goods and services provided by the society have also increased. On January 18, 2016, in a speech at a special seminar for major leading cadres at the provincial and ministerial levels to study and implement the spirit of the Fifth Plenary Session of the 18th CPC Central Committee, Xi Jinping pointed out that "the essence of the concept of sharing upholds the development thought of putting the people at the center and embodies the requirement of gradually achieving prosperity for all."[2] The basic purpose of strengthening society building and social governance is enjoying together, benefiting the broad masses and gradually achieving prosperity for all. An important guarantee for building a moderately prosperous society, maintaining social fairness, achieving social justice and forming social harmony lies in promoting the fair distribution of public goods and public services, and advancing the enjoyment of basic public services for all and on an equal footing. To achieve that the fruits of social development are shared by everyone necessarily requires the society to continuously provide more and better public goods and to continuously equalize the provision of basic public services. Otherwise, the fruits of development shared by all will be hollow and deviate from its original purpose.

---

2   Comrade Xi Jinping's Remarks at the Symposium on Learning and Implementing the Spirit of the Fifth Plenary Session of the 18th CPC central Committee for Leading Cadres at Provincial and Ministerial Levels (January 18, 2016), *People's Daily,* May 10, 2016, p. 2.

Adhering to "putting people at the center", promoting fairness and justice, enhancing people's welfare and gradually advancing and achieving prosperity for all are the starting point and stopover point of the society building and social governance in China. When presiding over the 28th group study session of the Political Bureau of the CPC Central Committee, Xi Jinping emphasized: "We should adhere to enhancing people's welfare, promoting the human's comprehensive development, and make steadily advancing toward prosperity for all into the starting point and stopover point of economic development." In the face of new situations and new tasks the CPC Central Committee with Comrade Xi Jinping as the core, being brave in practice, change and innovation and having foresight and farsightedness, has advanced and strengthened society building and social governance, pushed forward the smooth progress of the society building and social governance in China and achieved fruitful results and great achievements. In summarizing the work of the past five years in the report of the 19th CPC National Congress, Xi Jinping emphasized: "Our vision of making development people-centered has been acted on, a whole raft of initiatives to benefit the people has seen implementation, and the people's sense of fulfillment has grown stronger."

Adhering to the guidance of the Thought on Socialism with Chinese Characteristics for a New Era, China has enhanced people's welfare by strengthening society building and social governance. Since entering the new century, especially since the convening of the 18th CPC National Congress, with the rapid growth of the national economy, various social conflicts and social problems have emerged. Therefore, China needs to strengthen the society building and social governance, and push forward the rapid development of society building and social governance. During his inspection and research in Zhejiang Province, Xi Jinping pointed out: "A good society should be full of vigor, harmony and order at the same time. Society building should be based on the basic principle of joint construction and sharing. The basic principle is to plan systematically in terms of institutions, mechanisms, systems and policies to safeguard and improve people's wellbeing. We should insist on doing what the masses want us to do. We will do our best and do what we can, and send more charcoal in the snow, so that all the work will be unified in terms of desire and effect." In recent years, China has been relatively rich in social public goods, and the level and parity of basic public services have been significantly improved. Education is developing rapidly, and free compulsory education in urban and rural areas has been fully realized. The basic medical and health care system in urban and rural areas has been initially established, universal health coverage has been basically achieved, and the construction of a healthy China has made great achievements. The new social assistance system has basically taken shape, the urban and rural basic pension insurance system has been fully established, and the social security system has been built with remarkable results. The society building in China is continuously being advanced, the governance of the Chinese society is continuously being innovated, and the whole society basically maintains a harmonious, stable and orderly development, with people living and working in peace and contentment and the overall national strength becoming stronger day by day.

According to the new deployment of society building and social governance, as one of the important elements of the "five-pronged" integrated plan of Socialism with Chinese Characteristics for a New Era, the basic direction of China's reform and development to strengthen and carry forward society building and social governance lies in further deepening the social system reform, carrying forward institutional innovation in the social field, forming a scientific and effective social governance system, improving the supply capacity of public products, advancing the equalization of basic public services, better safeguarding and improving people's wellbeing, continuously promoting social fairness and justice, continuously deepening the reform of the income distribution system and promoting the gradual achievement of prosperity for all in the whole society, so as to build a well-off society as soon as possible. When summarizing the work on people's wellbeing in the past five years in his report to the 19th CPC National Congress, Xi Jinping pointed out: "Decisive progress has been made in the fight against poverty: more than 60 million people have been lifted out of poverty, and the poverty headcount ratio has dropped from 10.2% to less than 4%. All-round progress has been made in the development of education, with remarkable advances made in the central and western regions and in rural areas. Employment has registered steady growth, with an average of over 13 million urban jobs created each year. Growth of urban and rural personal incomes has outpaced economic growth, and the middle-income group has been expanding. A social security system covering both urban and rural residents has taken shape; the level of people's health and medical and health care have been significantly raised. Solid progress has been made in building government-subsidized housing projects to ensure basic needs are met. Social governance systems have been perfected; law and order has been maintained; and national security has been comprehensively enhanced." The achievements of the society building and social governance in China have been recognized by the international community. "China's level of economic and social development has increased in all respects. China has solved the problem of feeding and clothing 1.3 billion people; reduced poverty by more than 700 million people, accounting for more than 70 percent of the total number of people reduced globally, and has taken the lead in achieving the Millennium Development Goal of halving poverty, making a great contribution to the cause of human poverty reduction. China has provided employment for 770 million people, achieved full coverage of 9-year compulsory education, and initially formed the world's largest universal health coverage system and social security system, winning the international 'Award for Outstanding Achievements in Social Security'. *The National Human Development Report 2016: China* released by the United Nations praised China as 'the fastest growing country in the past 30 years'."[3] "China will complete the target of poverty alleviation on schedule and build a moderately prosperous society in an all-round way, which will not only benefit Chinese people, but also make a great contribution to the global cause of poverty alleviation." Frédérick Douzet, the director of the Institute of geopolitics at the University of Paris Eight in France, said that China's achievements in the 13th Five-Year Plan stemmed from its institutional advantage of "concentrating on major tasks". "Whether it is for the people of the whole country to fight the epidemic together or to promote the steady resumption of work and production, the Chinese people have always been united and support social progress. China adheres to the principle of taking people's well-being as its greatest goal and has gathered great development momentum."[4]

---

3   Li Baodong, China Will Resolutely Follow the Road of Human Rights Development with Chinese Characteristics, *People's Daily*, December 10, 2016, p. 11.
4   Gong Ming, et al., Opportunities for China's Development in The World: Positive Comments by the International Community on China's Economic and Social Development Achievements During the 13th Five-Year Plan Period, *People's Daily*, October 4, 2020, p. 3.

Contents

PREFACE
Strengthening Society Building and Enhancing People's Welfare   i

CHAPTER ONE
**IDEATIONAL AND THEORETICAL BASIS OF
THE SOCIETY BUILDING IN CHINA   1**

   I. Marx and Engels' ideas of society building   2

   II. Mao Zedong's ideas of society building   8

   III.Theories of society building after Reform and Opening-up   15

CHAPTER TWO
**IMPROVING THE UNIVERSAL LEVEL OF
EDUCATION AND HEALTH   35**

   I. Running a modern education that people are satisfied with   36

   II. Advancing the construction of a healthy China   51

CHAPTER THREE
**SAFEGUARDING AND IMPROVING
PEOPLE'S WELLBEING   69**

   I. Advancing giving priority to the development of social employment   70

   II. Increasing the residents' income in a shared development   81

   III.Perfecting the social security system covering urban and rural areas   89

CHAPTER FOUR
**BUILDING A SOCIAL GOVERNANCE SYSTEM
WITH CHINESE CHARACTERISTICS**			**103**

I.	Strengthening the construction of a social governance system 104

II.	Building the basic public services system			117

III.	Basic formation of a modern social organization system		120

IV.	Innovating the social governance system			127

CHAPTER FIVE
**STRENGTHENING AND INNOVATING
SOCIAL GOVERNANCE**			**135**

I.	Perfecting the system for preventing and resolving social conflicts 136

II.	Innovating and perfecting the social credit system			142

III.	Establishing and improving the public safety system		151

IV.	Establishing a national security system			170

CONCLUSION

Chapter One

Ideational and Theoretical Basis of the Society Building in China

Since the 18th CPC National Congress, the theory and practice of society building and social governance have been based on Marx and Engels' ideas of society building and Mao Zedong's thoughts about society building. Marx and Engels' theories contain abundant ideas of society building, which are the theoretical basis of China's society building. Mao Zedong's thoughts about society building are the ideational and theoretical basis for the society building carried out in the new stage of China's Reform and Opening-up. Since the Reform and Opening-up, Chinese Communists have continuously advanced and strengthened the society building, achieved fruitful results in society building and a series of theories of society building have been formed. Among them, contents such as "ultimately achieving prosperity for all", "advancing human's comprehensive development", "building a harmonious society with human as its foundation" and "leading the people to create a happy life" are directly or indirectly derived from Marx', Engels' and Mao Zedong's ideas of society building. The theories of society building since China's Reform and Opening-up, together with Marx', Engels' and Mao Zedong's and other proletarian revolutionaries' ideas of society building, have formed the ideas and theories of China's society building and social governance in the new era.

I.   Marx and Engels' ideas of society building

Marx and Engels' basic theories about the future society contain abundant ideas of society building, which provide the basic ideational support for the society building in China at present. Marx and Engels' ideas of society building mainly include the idea that the future society is an "association of free men", that in an "association of free men" the state power is reabsorbed by the society, the means of production are commonly appropriated by the whole society, human obtains free and comprehensive development and the society is in a sustainable state of harmony.

1. "Association of free men"

Marxism is of great vision, impressive insight and lofty aspirations. As to the future society, Marx and Engels described it as: "In place of the old bourgeois society, with its classes and class antagonisms, we shall have an association, in which the free development of each is the condition of the free development of all."[1] Marx and Engels' idea that the future society is an "association of free men" is not only the basic starting point of Marxist theory, but also a high-level summary of the ultimate destination of the future society by Marxism. The association of free men is the ultimate aim of Marx and Engels' future society. Marx and Engels believe that the human society in the future will gradually form an association of free men, which will ensure that each individual lives a carefree and happy life on the basis of free and comprehensive development. In such an association of free men, the society will reabsorb the state power, the whole society will commonly appropriate the means of production, and each individual will develop freely and comprehensively. The association of free men is the future communist society.

2. Reabsorption of the state power by the society

Engels pointed out: "Society, which will reorganize production on the basis of a *free and equal association of the producers*, will put the whole machinery of state where it will then belong: into the museum of antiquities, by the side of the spinning-wheel and the bronze axe."[2] It can be seen from this discussion that in the future association of free men, all the state machinery will become

---

1   *Marx and Engels Collected Works*, Vol. 6, 2010, Lawrence and Wishart, p. 506.
2   *Marx and Engels Collected Works*, Vol.26, 2009, Lawrence and Wishart, p. 272.

a product of history, that is, the state will return to the society. In the field of vision of Marx and Engels, classes, state, political power and so on are all of historical nature. In the future association of free men, the state will wither away with the disappearance of classes, the intervention of state power in social relations will gradually become redundant in various fields and cease on its own, and the society as a whole will gradually evolve into an autonomous and self-governing body. Therefore, a new type of social relations and social forms are formed in the society as a whole. Here, people will focus on the leadership of the production process and on the management of things. The society reabsorbs the state power, pays attention to social organization and social management, forms an association of free men, and enters the communist society.

3. Common appropriation of the means of production by the whole society

Marx and Engels believe that in the future communist society, the whole society will jointly appropriate the means of production, which is the economic basis for the existence of communism and also the basic guarantee for human's free and comprehensive development. After the communist society realizes the common appropriation of the means of production by the whole society, the production management of the whole society will be carried out in a planned, organized and systematic manner according to the basic situation of the natural resources of the whole society and the needs of the members of the whole society, so as to produce social products for the consumption of all members of the society to meet the consumption needs of people. With the tremendous growth of social productive forces, the communist society will eventually realize for all members of the society from each according to his ability, to each according to his needs. People will develop freely and comprehensively, and live carefree and happy lives. Marx and Engels believed that capitalist society has its inherent basic contradiction, which is the contradiction between the socialization of production and the private appropriation of the means of production. The basic contradiction of the capitalist society cannot be overcome by the capitalist society itself. The only way to overcome the basic contradiction of the capitalist society is to overthrow the private ownership system of the capitalist society and achieve the common appropriation of the means of production by the whole society. Marx clearly pointed out: "The philosophers have only interpreted the world, in various ways; the point is to change it."[3] Here, Marx believed that changing the world was more important than interpreting the world, and therefore Marx issued a call for "proletarians of all countries, unite", defeat capitalism, build socialism, and ultimately realize communism. To sum up, Marx and Engels believed that capitalist society is the entrance to the future society, and that the future communist society is based on the common appropriation of the means of production in the capitalist society by the whole society. The common possession of the means of production by the whole society is the economic basis for the achievement of the lofty aim of Marxism – the association of free men.

4. Human's free and comprehensive development

Engels once elaborated that in an association of free men "every member of it can develop and use all his capabilities and powers in complete freedom and without thereby infringing the basic conditions of this society"[4]. From this we can see that the association of free men is both the ultimate aim of the future society, and also the fundamental guarantee for human's free and comprehensive development in the future society. The ultimate aim of realizing a communist society in the future is to achieve human's free and comprehensive development. Human's free and comprehensive development is not only the ultimate ideal pursuit of the founders of Marxism, but also the ultimate practical goal of realizing an association of free men in the future. In the future association of free men, the fundamental form of social practical activity carried out by human beings is labor and labor becomes human's prime want. Here, after labor has become human's prime want, the social wealth flows abundantly, thus effectively satisfying human's material needs of life. Meanwhile, the socially necessary labor time is greatly shortened, and human's free time will enormously increase, thus men will become free men. Free men with material security will have enough energy and more free time to be engaged in scientific research, self-education, artistic appreciation and any other social activity they are interested in, so that human's physical strength, mental strength and abilities in the association of free men will be fully developed, and human's free and comprehensive development will become an actual possibility. By means of "the free development of each is the condition for the free development of all"[5] proposed

---

3   *Marx and Engels Collected Works*, Vol.5, 1975, Lawrence and Wishart, p. 9.
4   *Marx and Engels Collected Works*, Vol.6, 2010, Lawrence and Wishart, p. 97.
5   *Marx and Engels Collected Works*, Vol.6, 2010, Lawrence and Wishart, p. 506.

by Marx, the future society will ultimately achieve the highest goal of the Marxist society building – ultimately achieving and guaranteeing human's free and comprehensive development by means of realizing "the association of free men". Xi Jinping also pointed out conclusively: "According to Marx and Engels' vision, the communist society will eliminate the opposition and difference between classes, between urban and rural areas, between mental work and physical work, implement from each according to his ability, to each according to his needs, truly realize social sharing and achieve the free and comprehensive development of each individual"[6].

5. Idea of harmonious society

Marx and Engels' expositions on harmonious society still shine with dazzling theoretical brilliance, and is a rare theoretical treasure of society building, which still has valuable guidance in the actual society building practice. "Harmony" is the basis of Marxist theory and practice, and it is the basic condition of the existence of human life. Marx and Engels' idea of harmony means that contradictions will not be extinguished in natural and social life, and contradictions need to be consciously regulated by human. Human needs to promote the evolution of nature and their own development on this basis, which is an active and dynamic harmony. Marx and Engels believe that the harmonious society mainly manifested in the two aspects of the harmony between human and nature and the harmony of social relations between human and human.

Let's start with the first aspect, the harmony between human and nature. Marx and Engels attached great importance to harmony between human and nature. Marx and Engels believed that the harmony between human and nature is the realm of the unity of matter and me and the harmony of mind and matter achieved by human's active transformation of the objective world, is the basis for human to have a footing and the level representing human's own development. As for the relations between human and nature, they believed that human is the unity of the activity and passivity, calling for the initiative spirit of the subject. They emphasized the necessity and possibility of human's subjective choice and believed that the human's freedom is the freedom to action, while harmony is the realm of the unity of matter and me and the blend

6   Comrade Xi Jinping's Remarks at the Symposium on Learning and Implementing the Spirit of the Fifth Plenary Session of the 18th CPC Central Committee for Leading Cadres at Provincial and Ministerial Levels (January 18, 2016), *People's Daily*, May 10, 2016, p. 2.

At Tianxin Village, Dapo County, Qiongshan District, Haikou City, Hainan Province, for more than 20 years, birds and villagers have got along like relatives. The photo shows a group of middle school students who are going to put a wild bird into nature after its recovery.

of mind and matter achieved by the active transformation of the world. Marx believes that nature is also a part of human life and human activities, and in terms of the human body, human must rely on their material products in order to live. Marx affirms the unity and harmony between human and nature on the basis of human life activities. Engels pointed out that humans must put themselves in the right position in nature, and correctly comprehend and master the laws of nature to regulate the relationship between human and nature. Along with the constant development of human's material production activities, the relations between human and nature changes, and tends to be unified. Human's protection of the natural environment is to protect mankind's own home. Therefore, with the development of production to meet their own needs, men must pay attention to maintain ecological balance, to consciously get along in harmony with the nature and to maintain the harmonious relations between human and nature.

Let's return to the second aspect, the harmony of social relations between human and human. Harmony in interpersonal relations is a means by which individuals can comprehensively develop their talents. The society should become the carrier of human's free development. In order to achieve social harmony, it is expected to establish interpersonal relations in which love is exchanged for love and trust is exchanged for trust. As for harmonious relations between human and human, Marx and Engels focus on contents such as the elimination of the antagonistic factors in the relations of production, the realization of economic equality and political freedom and elaborate on the question of social harmony. They believed that production can't be carried out by a single individual in isolation. In production, people should have a certain social relations and political relations. The mode of production is the core of interpersonal relations and reflects to the greatest extent the overall level of human mode of life. Marx and Engels believed that the productive activities are the mainstay of the human life activity and is the premise in making history. Marx said: "In production, men enter into relation not only with nature. They produce only by co-operating in a certain way and mutually exchanging their activities. In order to produce, they enter into definite connections and relations with one another and only within these social connections and relations does their relation with nature, does production, take place."[7] On the basis of identifying the relations of production as the mainstay of human's social relations, Marx and Engels' thinking about the harmony of human society always grasped this key. From the above analysis, it is not difficult to see that in the theory of Marx and Engels, "harmonious society" is another expression of the word communism. The essence of the future society revealed by Marx and Engels is human's free and comprehensive development as well as the harmonious progress of human and nature, which is not only the ideal goal of human society, but also the inevitable trend of the development of human history. Human society is to build a harmonious society that guarantees the free and comprehensive development of each individual.

In a word, the main purpose and ultimate pursuit of Marx and Engels' theoretical thinking on society building is to establish an "association of free men". In such an association the state power is reabsorbed by the society, the means of production are appropriated by the whole society, human obtains free and comprehensive development, a harmonious society is formed, and the communist society is achieved.

---

7 *Marx and Engels Collected Works*, Vol.9, 2010, Lawrence and Wishart, p. 211.

II. Mao Zedong's ideas of society building

The victory of the new democratic revolution and the success of the socialist revolution have provided China with the institutional environment and political guarantee for society building. After China has entered the historical period of socialism, how to carry out society building well has not only become a new subject facing the Communist Party of China and the People of all ethnic groups in China, but also an important key to test the wisdom of Chinese people and governance capacity of the Communist Party of China. According to the principle of seeking truth from facts and proceeding from reality, Mao Zedong combined the basic principles of Marxism with the concrete practice of the society building in China and pointed out that the society building in China should proceed from China's national conditions and adhere to its own path. Mao Zedong's thoughts on society building mainly include the following contents:

1. "Putting the masses at the center"

Mao Zedong was a great Marxist who consistently adhered to applying the basic principles of Marxism to the process of Chinese revolution and society building. The masses are the creators of history, which is one of the basic principles of Marxism, and Mao Zedong applied this basic principle to the society building in China and condensed it into "putting the masses at the center" in the society building in China. "Putting the masses at the center" is the core idea of Mao Zedong on the society building in China, which has been running through the process of the society building in China and has become a red line and the main line of the society building in China.

Mao Zedong gave a comprehensive, systematic and profound exposition on "putting the masses at the center" in the society building in China. Mao Zedong pointed out: "Another hallmark distinguishing our Party from all other political parties is that we have very close ties with the broadest masses of people. Our starting point is to serve the people whole-heartedly and never for a moment divorce ourselves from the masses, to proceed in all cases from the interests of the people and not from the interests of individuals or groups, and to understand the identity of our responsibility to the people and our responsibility to the leading organs of the Party."[8] Here, Mao Zedong pointed out the hallmark distinguishing Chinese Communists from other political parties, the purpose of the Communist Party of China as well its starting point, and emphasized that the Party should "put the masses at the center" in the society building in China. Putting the masses at the center and serving the people whole-heartedly are the fundamental starting point and foothold of the Party, the stopover point and destination of the society building in China. Mao Zedong's idea of "putting the masses at the center" in the society building in China is also embodied in the mass line of the Party. The mass line of the Party refers to "everything for the masses, reliance on the masses in everything, and from the masses, to the masses". This mass line embodies both Mao Zedong's outlook on the masses and the basic idea of having a footing on the masses in the society building in China and is an important guiding idea for the Party to carry out mass work and guide the society building in China. Therefore, Mao Zedong pointed out conclusively: "People, only the people, are the driving force creating world history."[9] Mao Zedong also emphasized: "The supreme test of the words and deeds of a Communist is whether they conform with the highest interests and enjoy the support of the overwhelming majority of the people."[10] Therefore, in the process of advancing the society building in China, Mao Zedong formed a complete set of ideas of society building "putting the masses at the center". The starting point of this set of ideas lies in constantly improving the masses' life, basing oneself on the masses themselves, gradually building a better and more beautiful Chinese society, so that the masses can live a happier life.

2. "Caring for the masses' life"

The society building idea of "caring for the masses' life" embodies the mode of realization of Mao Zedong's idea of society building in China. If we say that "putting the masses at the center" is the starting point and foothold of Mao Zedong's idea of society building in China and the stopover point and destination for the Chinese Communists to carry out society building in China, then the mode of realization of this destination is "caring for

---

8   *Selected Works of Mao Zedong*, Vol.3, People's Press, 1991, pp. 1094-1095.
9   Ibid., p. 1031.
10   Ibid., p. 1096.

the masses' life". Mao Zedong believed that the society building in China must be established on serving the people whole-heartedly, attaching great importance to safeguarding the interests of the masses, continuously caring for the hardships of the masses, constantly improving the lives of the people, and insisting on promoting the happiness of the people. Mao Zedong once emphasized: "Increase agricultural production, safeguard the interests of the workers, establish co-operatives, develop trade with outside areas, and solve the problems facing the masses – food, shelter and clothing, fuel, rice, cooking oil and salt, sickness and hygiene, and marriage. In a word, all the practical problems in the masses' everyday life should claim our attention"[11]. Here, we can see clearly that in Mao Zedong's vision, society building is to solve the concrete problems in the masses' practical life. Constantly solving the masses' problems of food, shelter and clothing, fuel, rice, cooking oil and salt, sickness and hygiene, and marriage is the concrete embodiment of the Chinese Communists' "caring for the masses' life" and also the concrete mode and way to achieve the ending of "putting the masses at the center".

After the founding of the People's Republic of China, Mao Zedong practiced and explored a series of problems on how to carry out society building, how to develop the national economy and how to improve people's living standards and achieved better results. In 1959, Mao Zedong pointed out: "It is necessary to arrange people's clothing, food, shelter, daily needs and transportation, which is a problem of stability and instability of the 650 million people."[12] In 1962, under the leadership of Mao Zedong, China's national economic development strategy basically formed the basic idea of "paying attention to food, clothing and daily necessities first and achieving development of agriculture, light and heavy industry" in the whole society. It can be seen that Mao Zedong attached special importance to solve the society building in China well, to develop the national economy well and to improve the people's concrete living standards. He was also very concerned about the masses' life, about constantly meeting the masses' basic daily needs of life and constantly promoting the masses to live a happier and better life.

---

11   *Selected Works of Mao Zedong*, Vol.1, People's Press, 1991, pp. 136-137.
12   *Collected Works of Mao Zedong*, Vol.8, People's Press, 1999, p. 78.

3. "Improving people's life"

Mao Zedong attached immense importance to improving people's life. During the lengthy period of Chinese revolution and society building, Mao Zedong considered it very important to improve people's life. As early as the March 1949, at the Second Plenary Session of the 7th CPC Central Committee, Mao Zedong clearly pointed out: "If we know nothing about production and do not master it quickly, if we cannot restore and develop production as speedily as possible and achieve solid successes so that the wellbeing of the workers, first of all, and that of the people in general is improved, we shall be unable to maintain our political power, we shall be unable to stand on our feet, we shall fail."[13] At the beginning of the founding of the People's Republic of China, Mao Zedong emphasized: "We should make proper readjustments in industry and commerce so that factories can resume operation and the problem of unemployment can be solved, and we should provide 2,000 million catties of grain for the jobless workers and gain their support. When we reduce rent and interest, suppress the bandits and local tyrants and carry out agrarian reform, the masses of the peasantry will support us. We should also help the small handicraftsmen find ways to earn a living."[14] People's hearts is biggest politics. These ideas of Mao Zedong have strengthened and improved the then society building, raised the living standard of numerous workers and the people in general, won over the people's hearts in greatest number and guaranteed the then social stability. According to these important ideas, as early as the founding days of the People's Republic of China, the unemployment relief system was quickly established in enterprises. *The Labor Insurance Regulations of the People's Republic of China* implemented on March 1, 1951, has concretely stipulated the various systems such as employee health, old age, sickness, death, disability, medical treatment and collective insurance. *The Constitution of the People's Republic of China* adopted at the First Session of the First National People's Congress on September 20, 1954, explicitly stipulates that: "Working people of the People's Republic of China have the right to material aid in old age, and in case of illness and disability. To guarantee enjoyment of this right, the state provides social insurance, social

13   *Selected Works of Mao Zedong*, Vol.4, People's Press, 1991, p. 1428.
14   *Collected Works of Mao Zedong*, Vol.6, People's Press, 1999, p. 74.

relief and public health services and gradually expands these facilities."[15] Since then, China has also formulated a series of preferential regulations on social relief and social welfare, formed a relatively perfect social security system and provided the institutional basis for improving people's life. These ideas, institutions and legal provisions in the early years of the People's Republic of China both reflect Mao Zedong's society building idea of "improving people's life" and unfold the concrete practice of society building at that time, and are an important embodiment of the society building at the period of Mao Zedong. Strengthening society building and improving people's life achieved obvious results at that time. The broad masses of people lived and worked in peace and contentment, the society developed in a stable and orderly manner, the people's living standards were gradually raised, and the Communist Party of China won the support and backing of the great majority of the people.

4. "Attaching importance to the development of education and health care"

Education and health care are important aspects of society building. In the process of advancing the society building in China, Mao Zedong attached great importance to the development of educational and medical and health care undertakings. In terms of the development of the educational undertakings alone, after the founding of the People's Republic of China, under Mao Zedong's leadership, China gradually formed a relatively complete education system. Mao Zedong emphasized: "Education should emphasize popularization, not emphasize improvement and not overemphasize the quality."[16] Mao Zedong pointed out that people's governments at all levels should strive to "set up middle schools in towns and primary schools in villages" and that people's governments at all levels should make the realization of "compulsory education" and "free education" a key task. Mao Zedong also emphasized that thousands of colleges and universities should be built nationwide to form a complete Chinese education system. Although the economic hardship hit China at that time, Mao Zedong insisted on the development of mass education, and continuous investment

---

15   The Party Literature Research Office of the CPC Central Committee, *Selected Important Documents Since the Founding PRC*. Vol. 5, Central Party Literature Press, 1993, p. 540.
16   *Collected Works of Mao Zedong*, Vol.7, People's Press, 1999, p. 245.

in education. After the founding of People's Republic of China, the highest investment in the national education expenditure once reached 5% of the GDP. These thoughts on education and the practice of vigorously developing China's educational undertakings fully embody Mao Zedong's high attention on the development of China's education.

Mao Zedong also attached great importance to the development of China's medical and health care undertakings. After the founding of People's Republic of China, Mao Zedong vigorously strengthened the construction of medical and health care undertakings system and promoted the development of Chinese medical and health care undertakings. Under Mao Zedong's leadership, China has established a regular system of health care work. In 1965, Mao Zedong instructed to "shifting the focus of medical and health care work on rural areas", to "gradually establish hospitals, health centers, clinics and rural grassland medical teams, epidemic prevention stations, anti-syphilis stations and other health care sites in the central areas

The photo shows Dr. Wang, a barefoot doctor is seeing patients in his neighborhood in Shennongjia, Hubei Province, with his medicine box.

and densely-populated areas"[17]. Thus, a new situation of developing rural medical and health care undertakings has taken shape in China. In China's vast rural areas, hospitals were set up at the county level, health centers at the commune level, and health offices at the village level, and a more complete three-tier medical and health care infrastructure was built. In the vast rural areas, medical and health care undertakings have been creatively developed, rural cooperative medical care was actively carried out, grassroots medical personnel were vigorously trained, and rural barefoot doctors were trained. Under the guidance of Mao Zedong's idea of vigorously developing the medical and health care undertakings in China, the rural medical pattern of "small illnesses do not leave the village and big illnesses do not leave the countryside" and "wherever there are people, there is a doctor and medicine" has basically been realized in the vast rural areas of China. Under Mao Zedong's leadership, the health care undertakings made considerable progress in the society building in China. In the vast rural areas, the systems of "cooperative medical care", "rural health care station" and "barefoot doctors" have taken shape, effectively solving the peasants' medical and health care issue, and promoting the sustainable and stable development in the vast rural areas.

In a word, despite setbacks and mistakes Mao Zedong led the Chinese people to carry out society building. Having their footing on "putting the masses at the center", focusing on "caring for the masses' life", vigorously "improving the people's life", constantly paying attention to the development of China's educational and medical and health care undertakings, caring for the hardships of the people, improving the masses' life, and focusing on social management, Mao Zedong's ideas of society building laid a solid ideational basis for the society building during the period of Reform and Opening-up.

---

17   The Party Literature Research Office of the CPC Central Committee, *Selected Important Literature Since the Founding PRC*. Vol. 3, Central Party Literature Press, 1992, p. 435.

III. Theories of society building after Reform and Opening-up

The society building since China's Reform and Opening-up has gone through a historical process of gradual development, which is still in progress so far. The theories of society building since China's Reform and Opening-up are an important part of the theoretical system of socialism with Chinese characteristics, and have been gradually formed on the basis of the CPC's leadership of the Chinese people in the process of building socialism with Chinese characteristics and constantly summing up the valuable experiences of the society building. The theories of society building since China's Reform and Opening-up mainly include the theory of "ultimately achieving prosperity for all" formed in the new era of Reform and Opening-up by Deng Xiaoping, the theory of "advancing human's comprehensive development" guided by the important thought of "Three Represents" proposed by Jiang Zemin, the theory of "building a harmonious society with human as its foundation"[18] guided by the Scientific Outlook on Development proposed by Hu Jintao and the theory of "leading the people to create a happy life" proposed by Xi Jinping.

1. "Ultimately achieving prosperity for all"

After the Third Plenary Session of the 11th CPC Central Committee, China entered the new era of Reform and Opening-up pioneered by Deng Xiaoping. Deng Xiaoping led the Chinese people to carry out society building in China. In terms of national development strategy, Deng Xiaoping led the Chinese people to shift the focus of China's work to the construction of socialist modernization, established a national development strategy centered on economic construction, and gradually constructed the strategic goal of the "three-pronged" construction of socialist modernization with Chinese characteristics with prosperity, democracy and civilization as the core.

Deng Xiaoping's theory of society building is mainly covered in the achievement of the second great theoretical leap of combining Marxism with the practice of China's socialist construction – Deng Xiaoping Theory.

---

18 The English translations for *yi ren wei ben* made by Chinese authorities usually use the term "putting people first". – Ed.

"Deng Xiaoping Theory is the great theory that guides the Chinese people to triumphantly realize socialist modernization. In contemporary China, only Deng Xiaoping Theory, which combines Marxism with contemporary Chinese practice and the characteristics of the times, and no other theory can solve the problem of the future fate of socialism. Deng Xiaoping Theory is the Marxism of contemporary China, the inheritance and development of Mao Zedong Thought, and a new stage in the development of Marxism in China."[19] The main contents of Deng Xiaoping's society building mainly includes actively advancing the "three-step" development strategy in China, reaching a per capita income of US\$ 800 in the 20th century, the basic realization of moderate prosperity, and turning China into a moderately developed country in the mid-21st century. With Deng Xiaoping's "three-step" development strategy drew a grand blueprint for the Chinese people to move from poverty to sustenance, from sustenance to moderate prosperity, from moderate prosperity to modernization, and then to achieve the great rejuvenation of the Chinese nation. Deng Xiaoping' theories on the society building in China in the new era of Reform and Opening-up includes the following four main aspects:

First, the society building in China should proceed from the reality that China is and will remain in the primary stage of socialist society for a long time. In the late 1970s and early 1980s, with the Chinese society entering the period of Reform and Opening-up, Deng Xiaoping led the Chinese people to clearly recognize the condition and development stage of the Chinese society. Deng Xiaoping pointed out that China had a large population, less cultivated land per capita, a weak national foundation, 80% of which are farmers, and the per capita level of education was low. This was the basic condition of the Chinese society. Meanwhile, China's socialist system is still in its primary stage and the material civilization and spiritual civilization are in an underdeveloped stage. China needs to develop its productive forces vigorously and needs to do work well on building material and spiritual civilization to satisfy the growing material and cultural needs of the masses.

The theory of the primary stage of socialism includes two layers of meaning: first, Chinese society is already a socialist society, and China must adhere to but not leave socialism; second, China's socialist society is still in

---

19   *Selected Works of Jiang Zemin*, Vol. 2, 2006, People's Press, p. 264.

the primary stage. China must proceed from this reality and can't surpass beyond this stage. The first layer of meaning clarifies that the social nature of China at this stage is a socialist society; the second layer of meaning specifies that China's socialist society is still in the underdeveloped stage. This is a complete and inseparable scientific assertion. China's primary stage of socialism is a longer historical stage lasting one hundred years. At this stage, China's social productive forces are backward, its economic development is unbalanced, natural economy and semi-natural economy occupy a considerable proportion, the degree of the socialization of production is low, the commodity economy and the market economy are underdeveloped, etc. Therefore, the society building in China should proceed from the basic national situation that China is in the primary stage of socialism. The correct understanding of the theory of the primary stage of socialism is very important to do well at the society building in China and the Reform and Opening-up.

Second, the society building in China should take the people as the force to rely on and ultimate aim of society building. In China, it is a fundamental question to strengthen "whom to rely on and whom to serve" in the society building. Deng Xiaoping believes that, in terms of the force to rely on, strengthening the society building in China relies on the broad working class, peasant class and the intellectuals to succeed. Meanwhile, the fundamental aim of strengthening the society building in China is for the great majority of the people including workers, peasants and intellectuals. Deng Xiaoping emphasized that the society building in China must rely on the working class, peasant class and the intellectuals, must rely on the unity and cooperation of all nationalities, must rely on the broadest patriotic united front, and must rely on the great majority of the people.

Deng Xiaoping answered the question of how to strengthen the society building in China, and deeply explored the force to rely on in the society building in China and the ultimate goal of carrying out the society building in China. Deng Xiaoping pointed out: "None of the major tasks proposed by the Party can be accomplished without the arduous work of the great majority of the people."[20] The Chinese working class is the class foundation of the Communist Party of China and it must rely on the working class whole-heartedly to exert its master role in the society building. The masses

---

20 *Selected Works of Deng Xiaoping*, Vol.3, 1993, People's Press, p. 4.

of peasants are the most populous force to rely on in the society building in China. China's national conditions determine that the peasantry is not only the ally forces and main force of the new democratic revolution, but also the force to rely on in the society building in China. We should fully mobilize the enthusiasm and creativity of the masses of peasants and establish a consolidated worker-peasant alliance. Intellectuals are the part of the Chinese working class who possess more scientific and cultural knowledge and are mainly engaged in mental labor, are the representatives of the advanced productive forces, and who bear a great historical responsibility in the society building in China.

Deng Xiaoping attached great importance to the role of intellectuals in the society building in China. The clarification of the confusion in the early period of China's Reform and Opening-up started from the intellectuals first. At the National Science Conference held in March 1978, Deng Xiaoping emphasized: The Chinese intellectuals "are already intellectuals serving the working class and other working people. It can therefore be said that they are already part of the working class itself"[21], "such revolutionary intellectuals are a force our Party can rely on."[22] Deng Xiaoping also pointed out: "The key to achieving modernization is the development of science and technology. And unless we pay special attention to education, it will be impossible to develop science and technology. Empty talk will get our modernization nowhere; we must have knowledge and trained personnel. Without them, how can we develop our science and technology?"[23] Deng Xiaoping's theory on the force to rely on in the society building in China is rooted in the mass line of the Communist Party of China, that is "trust the masses, rely on the masses, from the masses, to the masses", fully unite all the forces that can be united and fully mobilize all the positive factors that can be mobilized to strengthen the society building in China.

Now that we have found the force to rely on in the society building in China, what is the fundamental purpose of the society building in China? The fundamental purpose of the society building in China is to help raise the living standards of the people. Deng Xiaoping pointed out that in China, the criterion of judgment to measure the merits and demerits of all

---

21   *Selected Works of Deng Xiaoping*, Vol.2, 1993, People's Press, p. 89.
22   Ibid., p. 93.
23   Ibid., p. 40.

work in China is the "Three Favorables", namely, whether it is favorable to the development of the productive forces of the socialist society, whether it is favorable to strengthening the comprehensive national power of the socialist country, and whether it is favorable to raising the living standards of the people. Among them, whether it is favorable to raising the living standards of the people is both the essential feature of the nature of the Chinese people and the starting point and the stopover point of the society building in China.

In a word, the great majority of the people are the force to rely on in the society building in China, and the ultimate aim of the society building in China is to raise the living standards of the overwhelming majority of the people.

Third, in the society building in China, we should exert the driving role of spiritual civilization based on paying attention to developing material civilization and adhere to the method of "grasping with both hands" of relying on material civilization and spiritual civilization. In order to do well in the society building in China, Deng Xiaoping put forward a series of theoretical viewpoints of "grasping with both hands, grasping firmly with both" and indicated the importance of adhering to "grasping with both hands" in the period of Reform and Opening-Up. The society building in China should grasp the economic and society building with one hand and combat various crimes with the other, grasp democracy with the one hand and legal system with the other, grasping material civilization with the one hand and spiritual civilization with the other and so on. These are the typical representatives of Deng Xiaoping's theory of "grasping with both hands". Deng Xiaoping's theory of "grasping with both hands" is one of the important guiding theories in carrying out society building as well as the construction in terms of economy, politics and culture in China. According to Deng Xiaoping's theory of "grasping with both hands", an important aspect of the society building in China is to give full play to the leading and driving role of spiritual civilization based on paying attention to developing material civilization.

One of the key points of the theory of "grasping with both hands" is to build a high degree of spiritual civilization in the society building. Using the basic principle of historical materialism, Deng Xiaoping scientifically pointed out on the basis of his experience in the society building in China: "The so-called spiritual civilization refers not only to education, science, and culture (this is totally necessary), but also to communist ideology, ideals, faith, ethics, discipline, revolutionary stand and principles, and the comradeship between man and man, etc."[24] This generalization of Deng Xiaoping reveals the connotation of two aspects of spiritual civilization, namely, education, science and culture and ideology and morality. Raising the people's educational, scientific and cultural and ideological and moral level is an important content of Deng Xiaoping's theory of society building. The scientific definition of the connotation of spiritual civilization lays a theoretical basis for how to carry out the society building in China.

As two basic aspects of spiritual civilization, education, science and culture and ideology and morality are organically unified and cannot be achieved without one another. What the construction of education, science and culture has to solve is the question of raising the quality of national scientific culture and the intellectual support for the society building. On the one hand, it must adapt to the development level of the social productive forces, on the other hand, it is also an important condition for the society building and improving the ideological and moral level of the members of the society, it is the basis of spiritual civilization. Ideology and morality are the soul and core of spiritual civilization. What the construction of ideology and morality has to solve is the issue of the spiritual pillar and spiritual motivation of individuals and the whole nation and society, as well as the direction of social development, thus determining the nature and direction of spiritual civilization and even the society building as a whole. The construction of ideology and morality plays an important role in guiding, promoting and guaranteeing the healthy development of the society building in China along the right track.

Fourth, the society building in China should be carried out in accordance with the essential requirement of socialism of "ultimately achieving prosperity for all". "What is socialism, and how we build socialism" is the basic theoretical question of chief importance that Deng Xiaoping constantly raised and repeatedly explored in the process of China's Reform and Opening-up and the society building in China. Without a clear understanding of this question, the development direction of the society building in China cannot be clarified, not to mention the consolidation and development of socialism.

---

24 Ibid., p. 367.

As Deng Xiaoping pointed out: "The question is what socialism is and how we build socialism. We have many of the lessons, the most important one, is to have a clear understanding of this question."[25]

According to the basic principles of Marxism, Deng Xiaoping summed up the practical experience of socialism and, after unremitting exploration and profound thinking, scientifically and incisively revealed the essence of socialism. Deng Xiaoping pointed out: "The essence of socialism is liberation and development of the productive forces, elimination of exploitation and polarization, and ultimate achievement of prosperity for all."[26] The theoretical generalization on the essence of socialism has laid a theoretical basis for the society building in China and development of socialism with Chinese characteristics, scientifically answered the basic theoretical question of chief importance of "What is socialism and how we build socialism", and pointed out that China's Reform and Opening-up must adhere to the socialist road, adhere to its own path, build socialism with Chinese characteristics, strengthen and carry out the society building in China, and ultimately achieve prosperity for all.

Proceeding from Deng Xiaoping's theory of the essence of socialism, the means of the society building in China is "liberation and development of the productive forces", and the mode and method of the society building in China is "elimination the exploitation and polarization", and the ultimate aim of the society building in China is to make the broad masses of Chinese people "ultimately achieve common prosperity". Deng Xiaoping's theory of the essence of socialism is the basic guideline for building the Chinese society.

In a word, Deng Xiaoping's theory of society building in the period of China's Reform and Opening-up is very rich in content and has a very strong practical pertinence. On the basis of correctly judging that Chinese society is in primary stage, Deng Xiaoping's theory of society building, by giving full play to the driving role of the construction of spiritual civilization, is to ultimately achieve common prosperity of the great majority of the people and to build China into a rich and powerful, democratic and civilized socialist country.

---

25   Ibid., p. 116.
26   *Selected Works of Deng Xiaoping*, Vol.3, 1993, People's Press, p. 373.

2. "Advancing human's comprehensive development"

After the Fourth Plenary Session of the 13th CPC Central Committee, Jiang Zemin put forward the important thought of "Three Represents". "Three Represents" means that the Communist Party of China must always represent the development requirements of China's advanced productive forces, the development direction of China's advanced culture and the fundamental interests of the broadest number of Chinese people. The important thought of "Three Represents" centrally reflects Jiang Zemin's exploration and development of the society building in China and socialism with Chinese characteristics. The important thought of "Three Represents" "creatively links the Party's construction with the development trend of today's world and contemporary China, with the self-improvement and development of China's socialist system, with the magnificent goals and tasks of realizing socialism with Chinese characteristics, gives the Party's nature and purpose, its guiding ideology and its tasks the content and the characteristics of the times, marking that the Party's understanding of the laws of the rule by a communist party, the laws of socialist construction and the laws of development of human society have reached a new theoretical height and opened a new realm for the development of Marxism."[27] With the guidance of the important thought of "Three Represents", Jiang Zemin has pushed forward the society building in China, and further enriched and developed the theory of the society building in China by advancing human's comprehensive development and the comprehensive development of the society.

First of all, the society building in China should take the fundamental interests of the broadest number of the people as its starting point and the stopover point. Jiang Zemin emphasized that the Communist Party of China should always represent the fundamental interests of majority of the broadest number of the Chinese people. The Party should achieve the representation of the broadest number of the people, "the most fundamental thing is to take the realization and protection of the interests of the broadest masses of the people as the starting point and stopover point of all our work, and strive to make the basic masses of workers, peasants and

---

27 The Party Literature Research Office of the CPC Central Committee, *Selected Important Literature After the 16th CPC National Congress*. Vol. 1, Central Party Literature Press, 2005, p. 358.

intellectuals enjoy the fruits of reform and development together. All the Party's guidelines and policies must be based on the highest standard of whether they meet the interests of the broadest masses of the people and the fundamental criterion of whether the broadest masses of the people are satisfied."[28] Representing the fundamental interests of the broadest masses of the people is inherently unified with representing the development requirements of China's advanced productive forces and the forward direction of China's advanced culture. This unity is not only a unity in theory and logic, but also a unity in practice. The development of advanced productive forces is the basic condition for the development of advanced culture and the realization of the fundamental interests of the broadest number of people. Meanwhile, the development of advanced productive forces is inseparable from the higher ideological and moral quality of the people and their educational, scientific and cultural level. In China, strengthening the society building is ultimately aimed at safeguarding and realizing the fundamental interests of the broadest number of people on the basis of developing advanced productive forces.

The masses are the creative subject of advanced productive forces and advanced culture, and the fundamental force in realizing their own interests. Meanwhile, the continuous development of advanced productive forces and advanced culture is, in the final analysis, aimed at meeting the growing material and cultural needs of the people and to continuously realizing the fundamental interests of the broadest number of people. As Jiang Zemin pointed out: "To always represent the fundamental interests of the overwhelming majority of the Chinese people, our Party must have its theory, line, program, principles, policies and all work to persevere in taking the fundamental interests of the people as the starting point and purpose, bring into full play people's enthusiasm, initiative and creativity, and enable the people to constantly obtain tangible economic, political and cultural benefits through continuous social development and progress."[29] With the fundamental interests of the broadest number of people as its value orientation, the CPC has both provided the basic impetus and the practical direction for the society building in China.

---

28   *Selected Works of Jiang Zemin*, Vol. 2, 2006, People's Press, p. 444.
29   *Selected Works of Jiang Zemin*, Vol. 3, 2006, People's Press, p. 279.

Second, the society building in China should take promoting a comprehensively developing and comprehensively progressing society as its general requirement. Jiang Zemin believed that the general requirement of the society building in China is to achieve comprehensive development and comprehensive progress of the Chinese society. Jiang Zemin pointed out: "Socialist society, as a brand-new social form in human history, is a society of comprehensive development and progress with economic construction as the focus."[30] Comprehensive development and comprehensive progress of the of society are the overall requirements of the society building in China. Jiang Zemin emphasized: "The various undertakings of socialist modernization that we carry out are the cause of mutual coordination and comprehensive development. Not only must the cause of economic construction go up, but the people's ideological and moral, scientific and cultural qualities, social order, and social atmosphere must be improved. Only in this way can we promote the overall progress of society and the comprehensive development of the entire social civilization."[31] Human development cannot be separated from the development of society, human development is the theme and core of social development, is the inevitable requirement of social development. The ultimate aim of social development should be anchored in human's comprehensive development. Achieving the comprehensive development and comprehensive progress in the society building in China can better promote human's comprehensive development.

Third, the society building in China should take promoting human's comprehensive development as its purpose and destination. Jiang Zemin's theory that the purpose and destination of the society building in China is to promote human's comprehensive development both inherits the Marxist idea of human's free and comprehensive development and combines with the characteristics of the times and the reality of the society building in China, enriching and perfecting the theory of human's comprehensive development. Jiang Zemin said: "All undertakings to build socialism with Chinese characteristics, and in fact, everything that we do should aim not just at meeting people's immediate material and cultural needs, but also at improving the qualities of the people, which is promoting human's comprehensive

30   *Selected Works of Jiang Zemin*, Vol. 2, 2006, People's Press, p. 258.
31   The Party Literature Research Office of the CPC Central Committee, *Selected Important Literature After the 13th CPC National Congress*. Vol. 3, Central Party Literature Press, 1993, p. 2080.

development. This is the essential requirement of Marxism regarding the building of a new socialist society. On the basis of developing the material and spiritual civilization of the socialist society, we should constantly advance human's comprehensive development."[32] Jiang Zemin's assertion on the society building in China is a new result of thinking about the basic theoretical question "What is socialism with Chinese characteristics and how we build socialism with Chinese characteristics?". For the first time in the literature of the Communist Party of China, Jiang Zemin has made human's comprehensive development the essential requirement for the society building in China. This new assertion was made on the basis of Jiang Zemin's in-depth study on the dialectical relationship between advancing human's comprehensive development and advancing the comprehensive development and comprehensive progress of the society in the practice of constantly advancing the society building in China. This new assertion strengthens the understanding of the Marxist idea of human's free and comprehensive development and emphasizes the values of the society building in China. By fully grasping and correctly applying the Marxist idea of human's free and comprehensive development, Jiang Zemin has elevated the theory of human's comprehensive development to a brand-new height. A comprehensive grasp and in-depth understanding of Jiang Zemin's theory of human's comprehensive development has far-reaching historical significance, brand-new practical significance and important theoretical significance for the correct understanding of the great practice of society building in China, for the advancement of human's comprehensive development at the primary stage of socialism with Chinese characteristics, and then for the gradual realization of the great rejuvenation of the Chinese nation.

In a word, the theory of society building in Jiang Zemin's important thought of "Three Represents" is rich in content. To sum up, Jiang Zemin's theory of society building takes safeguarding the fundamental interests of the great majority of the people as its starting point and stopover point, the comprehensive development and comprehensive progress of the society as its general requirement, the human's comprehensive development as its purpose and destination, unfolding the Party's sincere sentiment of always progressing at the same pace as the development of the times and sharing the same fate with the breath of the great majority of the people.

---

32   *Selected Works of Jiang Zemin*, Vol. 3, 2006, People's Press, p. 294.

Jiang Zemin has enriched and developed the theory of society building in China and laid the theoretical basis for the future society building in China.

3. "Building a harmonious society with human as its foundation"[33]

The main content in Hu Jintao concerning society building in China, in general, is to build a harmonious socialist society under the guidance of the Scientific Outlook on Development. "The Scientific Outlook on Development is a continuation and development of the important thoughts on development by the previous three generations of central collective leadership of the Communist Party of China and a concentrated expression of the Marxist world outlook and methodology concerning development. It is a scientific theory that is in the same line with Marxism-Leninism, Mao Zedong Thought, Deng Xiaoping Theory and the important thought of Three Represents that keeps abreast of the times. It is an important guiding principle for China's economic and social development and a major strategic thought that China must uphold and apply in developing socialism with Chinese characteristics."[34] The Scientific Outlook on Development emphasizes to take human as foundation, to achieve comprehensive, coordinated and sustainable economic and social development and to promote the comprehensive development of the economy, society and human. Hu Jintao emphasized that the society building in China shall be guided by the Scientific Outlook on Development and a socialist harmonious society should be actively built. Social harmony is the essential attribute of socialism with Chinese characteristics. Scientific development and social harmony are inherently unified, without scientific development there is no social harmony, and without social harmony it is difficult to achieve scientific development. Building a socialist harmonious society is a long-term historical task that runs through the whole process of the cause of socialism with Chinese characteristics, and is the historical process and social result of correctly handling various social conflicts on the basis of development. Proceeding from the society building in China, the harmonious society

33   See footnote 18.
34   Hu Jintao, *Hold High the Great Banner of Socialism with Chinese Characteristics and Strive for New Victories in Building a Moderately Prosperous Society in All Respects*, 2007, People's Press, pp. 12-13.

constructed in China is a socialist harmonious society jointly built and enjoyed by all people. Hu Jintao's theory on building a harmonious society in the society building in China mainly includes the following three aspects:

First, the society building in China shall adhere to taking human as its foundation and building a harmonious society. Hu Jintao believed that the basic direction of the society building in China is to build a socialist harmonious society and building a harmonious society shall adhere to taking human as its foundation. Adherence to taking human as foundation is to maintain and realize the fundamental interests of the great majority of the people, to take human's development as the fundamental purpose, to design and promote development based on the fundamental interests of the people, to guarantee the economic, political and cultural rights and interests of the people, to enable all the people to do their best and play their proper role, so as to realize human's comprehensive development. Taking human as foundation emphasized by Hu Jintao is to take the people's interest as the starting point and stopover point of all work and continuously meet the people's needs in all respects and achieve human's comprehensive development. Taking human as foundation is a thought concept, value orientation and scale of evaluation rooted in human. Hu Jintao pointed out: "Adherence to taking human as foundation means that human's comprehensive development shall be taken as purpose; the designing and promotion of development must be based on the fundamental interests of the people; the growing material and cultural needs of the people must be met continuously; and the economic, political and cultural rights and interests of the people must be guaranteed; and the fruits of the development must be shared by all people."[35]

The society building in China shall adhere to building a harmonious society based on taking human as foundation. A socialist harmonious society is a society full of creative vitality. It is both a society in which all people do their best and in which all people play their proper role. Building a socialist harmonious society requires the joint efforts of all members of the society and the unification of all the forces that can be united. To make the whole society full of creative vitality, it is necessary to release all creative aspirations favorable to social progress and let them be respected, bring creative vitality

---

35 The Party Literature Research Office of the CPC Central Committee, *Selected Important Literature After the 16th CPC National Congress.* Vol. 1, Central Party Literature Press, 2005, p. 850.

into play and let creative results be affirmed. Only in this way can we stimulate the creative spirit of the whole society and mobilize the enthusiasm of the whole society to create. This requires adherence to take human as foundation and putting people's interests first. Hu Jintao repeatedly emphasized: "We must adhere to exercising power for the people, building an emotional bond with the people, seeking benefits for the people, making every effort to handle difficult situations for them, persistently doing good deeds for the sake of the people."[36] Only by upholding the principle of putting people first, can we take people's interests as the prime want and ultimate goal of the society building, can we do everything to meet the needs of people and realize people's interests." Only by taking human as foundation can we take human as the starting point and stopover point of society building and do everything to meet human's needs and realize their rights and interests. Only in this way, it is possible to make all the people do their best and play their proper role and build a more harmonious society. Strengthening society building is to take human as foundation and to promote and achieve human's comprehensive development.

Second, the society building in China should adhere to the comprehensive development and coordinated development of the society. Hu Jintao pointed out that comprehensive development in the society building in China is to take economic construction as the center, comprehensively advance the economic, political and cultural construction and achieve the comprehensive development and coordinated development of the society. Comprehensive development can provide the basic guarantee for the construction of a socialist harmonious society and only comprehensively developing the society can constitute a "four-pronged" socialist harmonious society. Hu Jintao has elevated the society building in China to a brand-new height of "four-pronged". The past society building pattern in China mainly emphasized "three-pronged", emphasizing taking economic construction as the center and the "three-pronged" and coordinated of economic, political and cultural development. In September 2004, the *CPC Central Committee Decision on the Enhancement of the Party's Governance Capability* adopted at the Fourth Plenary Session of the 16th CPC Central Committee the concept of "society building" was used for the first time in the Party literature. Thus, Hu Jintao advanced the building of China from "three-pronged" to

---

36   Ibid., p. 371.

the stage of "four-pronged". "Four-pronged" is to give overall consideration to economic construction, political construction, cultural construction and social construction and develop them comprehensively and in a coordinated manner. "Four-pronged" which is founded on "three-pronged" gives prominence to the social construction. "Four-pronged" means to develop the four aspects of economic construction, political construction, cultural construction and social construction in all respects and in a coordinated manner, not one-sidedly, not focusing on one aspect and neglecting or weakening the others. Aside from the comprehensive development and mutual coordination of economy, politics and culture, the comprehensive and coordinated development of the society should strengthen the society building. We should keep the society itself stable and harmonious, and make the economy, politics, culture and society adapt to and promote each other; we should enhance social management and solve the problems appearing in social life through the self-perfection of the society; we should coordinate the economy, politics, culture as well as the society, and realize a coordinated "four-pronged" development by formulating scientific social development plans; we should raise the level of services and win the support of the masses through a higher level of services; we should enhance research on society building, adopt correct guidelines, policies and strategies, adjust the social structure, reform the social system and perfect the social operation mechanism, so as to gradually put the society building in China on the road of healthy, orderly and harmonious development.

Third, the society building in China should achieve comprehensive development under the guidance of taking human as foundation. Hu Jintao pointed out that under the guidance of the Scientific Outlook on Development, the society building in China should build a socialist harmonious society, advance the comprehensive development and the coordinated development of the society, adhere to taking human as foundation and ultimately achieving human's comprehensive development. To achieve human's comprehensive development, we should continuously improve the masses' level of material and cultural life and level of health based on economic development; we should guarantee the political rights and interests of the people, actively advance the course of political civilization, ensure that the people enjoy a wide range of political rights and freedoms in accordance with the law, and respect and safeguard human rights; we should vigorously develop the socialist culture with Chinese characteristics, strive to achieve the comprehensive development of human's ideological and spiritual life, continuously raise people's ideological and moral quality, scientific and cultural quality and health quality, guarantee the people's legal rights in education, employment, income, property and invention and creation and promote human's comprehensive development. Therefore, under the guidance of the Scientific Outlook on Development, the society building in China shall continuously achieve a harmonious socialist society, adhere to taking human as foundation, let all rely on the people, do all for the people and continuously promote and achieve human's comprehensive development.

In a word, the key content of Hu Jintao's theory of the society building in China lies in building of a socialist harmonious society under the guidance of the Scientific Outlook on Development. Its core lies in the adherence to taking human as foundation and its basic requirement lies in achieving comprehensive and coordinated development of the society building in China. The ultimate aim of advancing the comprehensive and coordinated development of the society is to promote and achieve human's comprehensive development, and ultimately achieve, maintain and develop the fundamental interests of the great majority of the people. Hu Jintao's theory on advancing the society building in China has not only broken through stereotypes, but also surpassed predecessors, and has actual and practical value and significance of theoretical guidance.

4. "Leading the people to create a happy life"

Since the 18th CPC National Congress, Xi Jinping attached great importance to the society building and social governance in China. "Taking human as foundation" is the core idea of the society building and social governance in China since the 18th CPC National Congress, and "leading the people to create a happy life is the unswerving goal of our Party" is the basic starting point and foothold of the society building and social governance in China since the 18th CPC National Congress. In January 2014, Xi Jinping went to Inner Mongolia for research and said: "We should place the people above all else in our hearts and make all efforts to solve the difficulties of the masses". Therefore, since the 18th CPC National Congress, the Chinese government has actively advanced the society building, focused on strengthening social governance and advanced social fairness and justice and people's wellbeing and happiness. The society building in China since the 18ᵗʰ CPC National Congress is no longer a one-sided social management by the government, but a social governance jointly governed by the government, whole society as well as the citizens. It is a historic leap forward for the society building in China that the society building in China advanced from the era of social management to the era of social governance.

The theories of society building and social governance since the 18ᵗʰ CPC National Congress are founded on the society building ideas of proletarian revolutionaries such as Marx, Engels and Mao Zedong, have a foothold on the theories of society building in China, are rooted in the great practice of the society building and social governance in China, and are continuously being developed and innovated. Marx and Engels' ideas of society building are the ideational basis for China to carry out society building, mainly including the idea that the future society is an "association of free men", that in an "association of free men" the state power is reabsorbed by the society, the means of production are commonly appropriated by the whole society, human obtains free and comprehensive development and the society is in a sustainable state of harmony. Mao Zedong's ideas about society building have pioneered society building in China during the period of socialist revolution and construction and include "putting the masses at the center", "caring for the masses' life", "improving people's life" and "attaching importance to the development of education and health care". Since the Reform and Opening-up, the Chinese Communists have led the Chinese people to continuously advance and strengthen society building, put forward and developed a series of theories on society building, and achieved fruitful results in society building. The content of the theories of society building since China's Reform and Opening-up mainly includes "ultimately achieving prosperity for all", "advancing human's comprehensive development", "building a harmonious society with human as its foundation" and "leading people to create a happy life".

Since the 18ᵗʰ CPC National Congress, the society building and social governance in China has entered a new stage of development, a series of theoretical results of have taken shape in society building and social governance, and the development of society building and social governance has been greatly pushed forward. China's achievements in society building and social governance since the 18ᵗʰ CPC National Congress include the following four aspects:

First, the universal level of education and health been improved in all respects. Specifically, China has made efforts to run a modern education that people are satisfied with and pushed forward the comprehensive, in-depth and sustainable development of China's education. To run a modern education that people are satisfied with, China has adhered to the concept of giving priority to developing education, advanced the balanced development of basic public education, pushed forward the integration of industry and education in vocational education, enhanced the ability of universities and colleges to generate innovators, accelerated the pace of the construction of a learning society, and enhanced the vitality of the education reform and development. In terms of improving people's level of health, China has advanced the construction of a healthy China, deepened the reform of the medical and health system, improved the universal medical insurance system, strengthened basic public health services, perfected the medical service system, ensured food and drug safety, and raised the level of maternal and child health care.

Second, the people's wellbeing has been improved in all respects. China has pushed developing social employment first, promoted shared development, increased residents' income, perfected the social security system covering urban and rural areas and effectively improved people's wellbeing. In terms of employment, China has advanced and achieved higher-quality employment, raised the capacity of public employment services, promoted the employment and entrepreneurship of college graduates, and created a fair employment environment. In terms of increasing residents' income, China has deepened the reform of the income distribution system, perfected the initial distribution mechanism, improved the redistribution adjustment mechanism, standardized the order of income distribution, and increased residents' property income. In terms of perfecting social security system covering urban and rural areas, the social insurance system has been perfected, the social assistance system has been improved, the social welfare system has been strengthened, and the development of the social charity undertakings have been advanced.

Third, a social governance system with Chinese characteristics has been built. The construction of a social governance system has been strengthened, the basic public services system has been built, a modern social organization system has taken shape, and the social governance mechanism has been innovated. Specifically, in terms of strengthening the construction of the social governance system, the way the Communist Party of China exercises leadership has been improved, a service-oriented government that satisfies the people has been constructed, the social collaboration, i.e., the assistance provided by non-governmental actors has been enhanced, the public participation has been advanced, and rule of law guarantees have been promoted. In terms of basic public services system, the main scope of the basic public services system has been established, the list system of the basic public services system has been established, the basic direction of the basic public services system has been specified, and the effective measures of the basic public services system have been implemented. In terms of realizing a modern social organization system, the separation of government and society has been strengthened, the clarification of powers and responsibilities has been advanced and law-based self-governance has been implemented. In terms of innovating the social governance mechanism, the concept of social governance has been innovated, social dynamics governance has been strengthened and social emergency governance has been perfected.

Fourth, social governance has been strengthened and innovated. The system for preventing and resolving social conflicts has been perfected, the social credit system has been innovated and perfected, a public safety system has been established and improved, and the national security system has been established. In terms of the perfection of the system for preventing and resolving social conflicts, the mechanisms to assess risks to social stability have been improved, the mechanisms to prevent and resolve social conflicts have been established, and the construction of a rule of law society has been advanced. In terms of the perfection and innovation of the social credit system, the credit information management system has been improved, the joint construction and sharing of credit information have been improved, the mechanisms to encourage keeping trust and punish breaking trust have been improved, and a credit services market has been cultivated and standardized. In terms of the establishment and improvement of a public safety system, the level of workplace safety has been raised in all respects, disaster prevention, mitigation and relief capabilities have been significantly improved, the system for preventing and controlling social security has been innovated, the construction of a system for emergency response to sudden incidents has been strengthened. In terms of the establishment of the national security system, the system and mechanisms to safeguard national security have been improved, the security and sovereignty of the political power have been safeguarded, economic security risks have been fended off and defused, and the construction of rule of law concerning national security has been strengthened.

To sum up, the society building and social governance since the 18th CPC National Congress are founded on the basis of society building ideas of proletarian revolutionaries such as Marx, Engels and Mao Zedong and on the theories of society building since China's Reform and Opening-up. Whether in the past or at present, maintaining and achieving the fundamental interests of the majority of the people has ever been the core of the society building and social governance in China. The society building and social governance in China lies in inheriting from predecessors, breaking through stereotypes, pioneering and innovating, continuously perfecting the guarantee of people's wellbeing, making the people enjoy better education, medical care, employment, continuously increasing the people's income and improving social security and so on. On this basis, the social governance is continuously strengthening and innovating and a perfect social governance system with Chinese characteristics is taking shape. On the basis of preventing and resolving social conflicts, the social credit system is being perfected, the public safety system is being improved, the national security system is being established, so that the society building and social governance in China will eventually reach the highest level of excellence.

Chapter Two

Improving the Universal Level of Education and Health

People's wellbeing is the key to governance, which the Chinese Communists always put in their heart, carry on their shoulders. People's wellbeing is closely linked with people's feelings and people's feelings condense people's strength. Working hard to safeguard and improve people's wellbeing is related to people's welfare and social stability. Xi Jinping pointed out that the general idea of safeguarding and improving people's wellbeing is "meeting basic needs, prioritizing key areas, improving institutions, and guiding public expectations", and its basic requirement is to pay attention to equal opportunities and focus on safeguarding the people's basic wellbeing. Since the 18th CPC National Congress, guided by the general idea of safeguarding and improving people's wellbeing as proposed by Xi Jinping, the Chinese government has done a good work in safeguarding and improving people's wellbeing. To safeguard and improve the people's wellbeing, the Chinese government has focused on relieving people's worries and difficulties, seeking their interests and increasing their welfare, so that they can share more and more fairly the enormous fruits of Reform and Opening-up and economic and social development. Education and health are two very important aspects of safeguarding and improving people's wellbeing. In accordance with Xi Jinping's general idea of safeguarding and improving people's wellbeing, in recent years, the Chinese government has focused on running a modern education that people are satisfied with, accelerated and advanced the construction of a healthy China, and improved the level of education and health of the entire population in all respects.

I.   Running a modern education that people are satisfied with

The 18th CPC National Congress pointed out: "Education is the cornerstone of national rejuvenation and social progress". At the National Ideological and Political Work Conference in Colleges and Universities, Xi Jinping also pointed out: "Strong education makes a country strong." The 19th CPC National Congress pointed out: "Strengthening education is fundamental to our pursuit of national rejuvenation. We must give priority to education, further reform in education, speed up its modernization, and develop education that people are satisfied with." Running a modern education that people are satisfied with is both the key area to safeguard and improve the people's wellbeing in the construction process of the Chinese society and the basic direction for China's education reform and development. Since the 18th CPC National Congress, the Chinese government has made earnest efforts and achieved remarkable results in running a modern education that people are satisfied. On the importance of education in the construction process of the Chinese society, Xi Jinping pointed out: "There are so many people in China. Once education is improved, talents will emerge like a blowout in the future. This will give the best competitive edge."[1] Therefore, the Chinese government is always committed to running a modern education that people are satisfied with.

"Paying attention to teachers is to attach importance to education, and winning education can win the future."[2] Safeguarding and improving people's wellbeing is the key area of society building in China, while running a modern education that people are satisfied with is the primary task to improve and safeguard people's wellbeing. Since the 18th CPC National Congress, the Chinese government has put running a modern education that people are satisfied with at the top its agenda of safeguarding and improving people's wellbeing, adhered to the concept of giving priority to the development of education, promoted the balanced development of the basic public education, improved the integration of industry and vocational education, enhanced the ability of universities to generate innovators,

---

1   *A Series of Important Speeches by General Secretary Xi Jinping* (2016 ed.), compiled by the Publicity Department of the CPC Central Committee, People's Press, 2016, p. 216.
2   China Has to Follow Its Own Path of Higher Education–On Learning and Implementing the Speech of the General Secretary Xi Jinping at a National Conference on Education in Political Philosophy at Institutions of Higher Learning, *People's Daily*, December 9, 2016, p .1.

accelerated the construction of a learning society and enhanced the vitality of education reform and development. All these reflect the high importance attached by the CPC Central Committee to educational undertakings and its firm determination to give priority to developing education and that it has truly pushed forward the in-depth progress of China's education reform and the development of China's education in the direction of modernization in all respects.

1. The concept of giving priority to developing education has been adhered to

In the process of advancing society building in China, the Chinese government has paid attention to safeguarding and improving people's well-being and adhered to the concept of giving priority to developing education. The concept of giving priority to developing education puts into effect the educational policy of the Communist Party of China in all respects. Xi Jinping pointed out: "China will resolutely implement the strategy of reinvigorating the country through science and education, and will always give priority to education. China will increase its investment in education, promote universal and life-long education, and build itself into a society in which people enjoy learning. Moreover, the country will work hard to ensure that every child has the opportunity to go to school, and enable its 1.3 billion people to enjoy a better and fairer education, so that they can acquire the ability to develop themselves, contribute to society and help others."[3] The fundamental task of China's education is cultivating virtue and nurturing personality, serving the overwhelming majority of the people and serving the modernization construction of China. Chinese education has trained a large number of builders and successors who are well developed morally, intellectually, physically and aesthetically. Adhering to the concept of giving priority to developing education, Chinese education has given prominence to enhancing human capacity for development, comprehensively raised the level of education modernization, focused on increasing the people's scientific and cultural literacy and sped up the construction of China's human capital powerhouse.

---

3   Xi Jinping Delivering a Video Message at the First Anniversary Ceremony of the UN 'Global Education First' Initiative, *People's Daily*, September 27, 2013, p. 3.

In China, the concept of giving priority to developing education has become a basic consensus of the whole society. The Communist Party of China and governments at all levels have effectively strengthened their guidance on the cause of giving priority to developing education, formulated strategies for the cause of giving priority to developing education, increased the investment guarantee of financial resources in the development of education as a priority, and promoted human resources and public resources to meet the development of education as a priority. In 2020, due to the impact of the epidemic and other factors, China's financial resources were very tight, but China's financial expenditure on education as a percentage of GDP continued to exceed 4%, and the central government's education expenditure still exceeded 1 trillion RMB. China is earnestly making good use of its precious funds, striving to run education satisfactory to the people, and holding up the hope of tomorrow. To implement the concept of giving priority to developing education, local governments at all levels have launched a "first-in-command" project prioritizing to the development of education, incorporated various indicators of prioritizing education development into the assessment system of governments and leading cadres at all levels, formed new mechanisms for giving priority to developing education, management all together and coordinated joint governance, implemented the concept of giving priority to developing education and laid a solid foundation for giving priority to developing a modern education. Qianyang County in Baoji City, Shanxi Province is very representative and typical for running big education in a small county and a rich education in a poor county.

Adhering to the strategy of giving priority to developing education, Qianyang County implemented the fundamental task of cultivating virtue and nurturing personality, increased the investment in the education of socialist core values, perfected the fund guarantee mechanism for compulsory education, raised the subsidies for the maintenance and renovation of primary and secondary school buildings, accelerated the development of vocational education and preschool education, and optimally upgraded the high-school education. Adhering to the concept of "running big education in a small county, rich education in a poor county, and strong education in a remote county", Qianyang county government vigorously supported the development of the education. The county treasury has included all the funds for compulsory education into its budget, and more than 20% of the new financial resources are spent on education every year. In 2015, the budget allocation for education in Qianyang County reached 270 million yuan (RMB), accounting for 26.2% of total financial expenditure, taking the lead in Baoji City to realize the major adjustment of school layout, the major popularization of preschool education, major reform of efficient classrooms, major improvement of campus environment and major balance of compulsory education, and reached all targets for the provincial-level education of a strong county, all standards for primary and secondary school construction, and the admission rate in the college entrance examination ranks in the forefront of counties and districts in the city. Qianyang County has won the province-level "Double High and Double Popular" award (high quality and high level of popularization of nine-year compulsory education, universal preschool education), became a qualified county with basically balanced development of national compulsory education and the 30th strongest county in the Shanxi Province, and the 6th strongest county in Baoji City for education. Under the great downward pressure of the economy, the financial department of Qianyang met basic needs, prioritized key areas, improved institutions, prioritized investment guarantees in education, strengthened fund management, enhanced the financial performance evaluation mechanism, improved the efficiency of fund use and ensured that its initiative work succeeded in one fell swoop, which has played a positive role in pushing forward the improvement of the education quality and economic and social development in Qianyang County.[4]

2. The balanced development of basic public education has been advanced

To develop the modern education that people are satisfied with, the Chinese government has strengthened the status and function of primary education and promoted the balanced development of the public education in urban and rural areas. On the position and development requirements of basic education, Xi Jinping pointed out: "Basic education is in a basic and leading position in the national education system. It is necessary to grasp its positioning, fully implement the party's education policy, and take measures

---

4   Pu Hongmei, The Small and Poor Qianyang County Has Invested Much in Education, *Western Finance and Accounting*, 2016(3).

from many aspects to make my country's basic education better and better."[5] About of the importance role and basic positioning of basic education, Xi Jinping emphasized: "Basic education is a cause of cultivating virtue and nurturing personality. We should resolutely boost the ideological, political and moral education, strengthen the education of socialist core values, guide students to promote their self-esteem, self-confidence, self-reliance and self-respect. Basic education is a foundational project for improving the quality of the nation. We should follow characteristics and laws of youth growth, solidly do a good job of the basic articles. Basic education should establish a strong outlook on talent, vigorously promote a quality-oriented education[6], encourage schools to teach their characteristics, encourage teachers to teach their styles."[7] To promote the balanced development of the basic public education resources in urban and rural areas, the Chinese government has increased the investment in education and national education funds were shifted to the old revolutionary base areas, the poverty-stricken areas and the remote countryside. As pointed out by Xi Jinping, when he went to Shanxi Province on the eve of 2015 Spring Festival to visit people and officials: "Education is crucial. The old revolutionary base areas and poor areas must still grasp the roots of development or pay attention to education. Do not let children lose on the starting line. We must pay attention to education and pay attention to basic education, especially basic education in old revolutionary base areas. Financial funds must be weighted towards this aspect." Therefore, in terms of funding guarantees for education, China has basically established a unified urban and rural funding mechanism for compulsory education which places emphasis on rural areas, and increased funding for public education in the central and western regions, remote or poor areas, and areas with concentrations of ethnic minorities.

About the different stages of basic education, Xi Jinping pointed out: "We should strengthen the support for basic education, improve preschool education, balance development of nine-year compulsory education and

---

5   Implementing the Party's Guiding Principle for Education in All Respects and Making Efforts to Make China's Basic Education Better and Better, *People's Daily*, Sept.10, 2016, p. 1.
6   The concept of *suzhi jiaoyu* is often translated as 'quality education' but it is closer in meaning to 'moral education' or even 'a well-rounded education' (including ideological and physical education). It involves an attempt to move away from test-oriented teaching toward critical thinking, problem solving, and other analytical skills. – Ed.
7   Ibid.

On June 25, 2015, at Zhijin County, Bijie Prefecture, Guizhou Province, nearly a thousand million yuan was invested in building schools for compulsory education so that the impoverished primary and secondary school students in mountainous areas, left-behind children can receive higher-quality compulsory education.

make senior secondary education universally available."[8] In recent years, the Chinese government has developed preschool education, helped make rural preschool education more accessible by encouraging the development of rural kindergartens open to all children, and carried out the three-year preschool education plan. In 2020, the gross enrollment ratio for children receiving three-year preschool education reached 85%. A balanced development of the nine-year compulsory education has been realized, appropriate measures to ensure that state-run schools that provide compulsory education comply with educational standards have been taken, the problems of school selection and reducing the burden of students' homework have been tackled without setting up key schools or key classes. The conditions in boarding schools as well as badly built and poorly operated schools have been improved, the regional layout of education institutions and services have been improved, extremely large class sizes in urban schools have been eliminated, a basic balance between schools in the same county in the

8   Ibid.

allocation of educational resources has been achieved, and the completion rate of compulsory education has been stabilized at 95% in 2020. The senior secondary school education has been made more universal and high priority has been given to waiving fees for senior secondary school students registered as economically disadvantaged students. In 2020, the gross enrollment ratio of senior secondary school education in China exceeded 90%.

In terms of the groups with disabilities, the Chinese government has increased the availability and quality of special needs education for groups with disabilities, and increased support given to such education. It has promoted the development of education for ethnic minority students, appropriately moved ahead with bilingual education, and strengthened bilingual teacher training.

In terms of faculty construction, the Chinese government has strengthened the construction of a principal-teacher exchange and rotation system, intensified the construction of the ranks of teachers, especially of rural teachers, implemented a support plan for rural teachers, and addressed structural, school level-specific, and regional teacher shortages through methods such as the provision of government-purchased teaching positions. It has improved the teaching environment in rural schools, the funding methods for education, and ensured that all students from financially disadvantaged families are covered.

3. The integration of industry and vocational education has been pushed forward

Vocational education is an important part of modern education. Strengthening modern vocational education and promote the integration of industry and vocational education is the development direction of modern vocational education. Since the 18th CPC National Congress, the Chinese government, in its efforts to running a modern education that people are satisfied with, has improved the modern vocational education system and strengthened the basic capacity construction of vocational education. The Chinese government has taken promoting "craftsman spirit" as its guide, attached importance to the development of modern vocational education system, pushed forward the perfection of the modern vocational education system, enhanced the basic capacity of the vocational education, and laid a solid basis for the development of modern vocational education. In

In recent years, Wenling City, Zhejiang Province, vigorously promoted education models with unique features such as integration of industry and education, school-enterprise cooperation and work-study combination, and and cultivated more than 3000 practical technical talents every year. The picture shows students of Wenling Vocational Secondary School displaying their hand-drawing skills.

the process of promoting the development of modern vocational education, China has gradually promoted the transformation of regular undergraduate colleges and universities with suitable condition to become applied and vocational-practice oriented, pushed forward the integration of some regular universities and modern vocational education, and enhanced the intellectual strength of the modern vocational education.

In terms of the cultivation of talents, China's modern vocational education has strengthened training models for applied talents which allow for the involvement of industry and vocational education as well as cooperation between schools and enterprises, advanced training models for technical skills, and promoted two-way exchanges between faculty members from vocational schools and technical staff members from enterprises. As emphasized by Xi Jinping: "The more forward times pass, the greater the importance of knowledge and talent is; the more prominent the status and role of education is. China develops in the best period of the history, but to achieve the 'two centenary' goals and the great goal of national rejuvenation, we must pay more attention to education, and strive to cultivate more and better talents to meet the needs of the party, country, people and the times."[9]

China's modern vocational education has also promoted the concrete alignment of professional settings, curriculum contents, teaching methods with the production practice, resulting in the effect of organic integration of teaching and practice in the vocational education. China's modern vocational education has also promoted mutual recognition, vertical mobility and horizontal exchange between vocational education and ordinary education, and pushed forward the organic integration of modern vocational education and regular education. To enhance the attractiveness of modern vocational education, the Chinese government has also phased in, based on classification, the waiving of tuition and miscellaneous fees at schools providing secondary vocational education, to attract people of the right age to actively participate in vocational training. Besides, the Chinese government has actively implemented the National Basic Vocational Training Package System[10] and pushed forward the standardization and institutionalization of vocational education and vocational training.

4. The ability of universities and colleges to generate innovators has been enhanced

To run a modern education that people are satisfied with and promote Chinese universities to become world-class universities, adherence to the Marxist theory as guidance is the most important ideological basis and earnest implementation of the educational line and policies of the Communist Party of China is the most important political guarantee. Xi Jinping pointed out: "To build better our colleges and universities, we should follow the guiding role of Marxism and thoroughly carry out the CPC's education policies. We should disseminate the scientific theory of Marxism, further improve

---

9   Ibid.

10   The vocational training package is the sum of vocational training resources integrating training objectives, training requirements, training contents, assessment syllabus, etc. developed for a certain occupation (job type) in order to strengthen the standardized management of vocational training, combined with the development of new economy, new industries and new occupations, based on occupational standards or enterprise job technical specifications. It is the work specification and guide for vocational training institutions to carry out government-subsidized vocational training services for workers. (*Notice of the General Office of the Ministry of Human Resources and Social Security on Advancing the Vocational Training Package Work*), MHRSS [2016] N.162, Effective Date: October 23, 2016.

Marxist education, and help students lay a scientific thinking for their life-long development."[11] The ability of universities and colleges to generate innovators is the key content of university education in modern education system. Xi Jinping pointed out: "The development of higher education is a key gauge of a nation's development and potential."[12] Therefore, paying great attention to the development of higher education is the most important for the modernized education people are satisfied with. Xi Jinping emphasized: "Managing higher education well affects a country's development and a nation's future. China's higher education should be closely focused on achieving the 'two centenary' goals and realizing the Chinese Dream of the great rejuvenation of the Chinese nation, and continuously cultivate a large number of outstanding talents with both political integrity and professional competence."[13] Since the 18th CPC National Congress, in order to run an education that people are satisfied with, the Chinese government has paid attention to enhancing the ability of universities and colleges to generate innovators and strengthening the construction of modern universities and colleges.

In order to promote Chinese universities to become world-class universities, the Chinese government has enhanced the ability of universities and colleges to generate innovators. Xi Jinping has pointed out: "Only those that can provide society with outstanding brains can become world-leading institutions. Therefore enhancing the all-round ability of Chinese universities and colleges to generate talent is the key to turning them into prestigious international brain banks, and the driver of all other work in higher education institutions."[14] "As a fresh troops of scientific and technological innovation, higher learning institutes must innovate their talent development schemes and teaching methods to cultivate more qualified and innovative talents for the country's development."[15] In recent years, the Chinese government has

---

11   Zhang Shuo, Put Ideological and Political Education throughout the Whole Teaching Process and Create a New Situation in the Development of China's Higher Education, *People's Daily* December 9, 2016, p. 1.

12   Ibid.

13   Xi Jinping Sent A Letter to Congratulate Tsinghua University on Its 105th Anniversary, *People's Daily*, April 23, 2016, p. 1.

14   Putting Ideological and Political Education throughout the Whole Teaching Process and Creating a New Situation in the Development of China's Higher Education, *People's Daily*, December 9, 2016, p. 1.

15   Xi Jinping: Wish the People of All Nationalities of the Country Health, Happiness and Auspiciousness, and Wish Improvement and Flourishing of Their Wellbeing, *People's Daily*, February 4, 2016, p. 1.

promoted the classified management of higher education and the overall reform of universities. It has optimized the layout of disciplines and specialties, reformed the mechanism of talents cultivation, carried out the training system of the integration between academic and applied talents, between general education and professional education, strengthened the practice teaching, and focused on fostering students' creativity and awareness for innovation and entrepreneurship. Xi Jinping emphasized: "We should ensure that universities and colleges remain harmonious and stable and nurture a rational and peaceful and harmonious mindset on campus. Humanistic care and psychological consultation should be offered to keep higher education institutions peaceful and harmonious. We should consistently build positive school spirits and academic attitude and ensure that every campus is well-managed, and its atmosphere is honest and upright."[16] Therefore, the Chinese government has promoted the construction of a modern university system, has perfected the internal governance structure of universities, has formed a good atmosphere for talent cultivation, has built world-class teaching staff and updated the teaching contents with new theories, new knowledge and new techniques. It has improved the system for ensuring the quality of higher education, thoroughly implemented the plan to invigorate higher education in the central and western regions and seen that more students from these regions and rural areas are able to enter key institutions of higher learning, ensured that all universities improve their capacity for innovation, and will adopt a coordinated approach to developing world-class universities and disciplines, and achieved initial results.

5. The construction of a learning society has been accelerated

The construction of a learning society is a great society building project in the field of education based on the present and with a long-term perspective. A modern and mature society should be a learning society, and only a society that continuously strengthens learning can provide a constant impetus for social development. In recent years, the Chinese government has vigorously developed continuing education, actively advocated the concept of "one is never too old to learn" in the whole society and laid a solid

---

16   Zhang Shuo, Put Ideological and Political Education throughout the Whole Teaching Process and Create a New Situation in the Development of China's Higher Education, *People's Daily*, December 9, 2016, p. 1.

ideological basis for China to build a learning society in which "everyone can learn, at anytime, and anywhere". In order to promote the implementation of the concept of lifelong learning, the Chinese government has also actively built a lifelong education and training system available to all members of society, creating a real learning environment for lifelong learning.

The Chinese government has encouraged the open sharing of all types of learning resources, ensure the success of open universities, develop online and distance learning, and integrate all kinds of digital learning resources to make them available to the general public. In terms of the construction of a concrete learning management and institutions for individuals, the Chinese government has also gradually promoted the establishment of a system for personal learning accounts and credits, made it easier for people to pursue continuing education and lifelong learning, formulate a national qualifications framework, and promote credit transfers and recognition of the learning outcomes of non-degree education and vocational skill grades. In addition, the Chinese government has steadily developed the senior citizen education, improved universities for senior citizens, formed a relatively perfect sunset education system, enriched the learning life of the senior citizens, truly extended the learning concept of "one is never too old to learn" to the sunset stage of people's life, and added rich practical content to the construction of a learning society.

6. The vitality of education reform and development has been enhanced

To develop a modern education people are satisfied with, the Chinese government needs to push forward the reform in the field of education and continuously strengthen the inner vitality of educational reform and development. Deepening educational reform is a comprehensive and systematic project and involves many aspects of education. The Chinese government is enhancing the vitality of the development of education and actively fostering China's educational undertakings in all respects precisely by continuously deepening the comprehensive reform of education.

In terms of students' cultivation, in recent years, the Chinese government has adhered to putting people at the center and putting students at the center, and the quality-oriented education for students[17] has made significant progress. As Xi Jinping pointed out: "Quality-oriented education is the core of education. Education should focus on putting people at the center and teaching students in accordance with their aptitude, focus on the integration of learning and application and unity of knowledge and action, focus on fostering students' innovative spirit and practical ability, and promote the comprehensive development of the students in moral, intellectual, physical and aesthetical aspects."[18] Therefore, the Chinese government has deepened the comprehensive reform in the field of education, strived to improve the quality of the education, implemented a quality-oriented education, enhanced students' sense of social responsibility, their awareness of rule of law, their spirit of innovation, and their ability to put ideas into practice, comprehensively strengthened education in sports, physical health, mental health, the arts, and aesthetics, and focused on cultivating students' interest in innovation and their scientific literacy.

In terms of examination, enrollment and instructional reform, the Chinese government has deepened the reform of the examination and enrollment systems as well as instructional reform and made continuous efforts to explore a set of examination and enrollment systems and instructional norms suitable for China's national conditions. At the junior high school and senior high school levels, the Chinese government has gradually administered the Academic Proficiency Test and the Comprehensive Student Assessment to junior and senior secondary school students, and promoted the development of students' comprehensive quality.

In terms of the management of teachers, the Chinese government has launched a nationwide reform of the professional title system for primary and secondary school teachers and improve teacher salaries and benefits. With a focus on of rural teachers, the government has thoroughly implemented the Special Recruitment Plan for Rural Teachers, the Tuition Free Normal College Students Program and the National Primary and Secondary School Teacher-Training Program, remarkably improved the overall quality of the ranks of teachers, and a large number of exemplary teachers have emerged. As Xi Jinping emphasized: "Teachers should be the

---

17   See footnote 6.
18   Implement the Party's Guiding Principle for Education in All Respects and Making Efforts to Make China's Basic Education Better and Better, *People's Daily*, Sept.10, 2016, p. 1.

guide for students to temper their character, be the guide for students to learn knowledge, be the guide for students to innovate their thinking and be the guide for their dedication to the country". Meanwhile, "teaching is the work of spreading knowledge, spreading ideas and spreading truth. Teachers are engineers of the human soul who undertake the mission of molding minds. Teachers should be respected, and the tradition of respecting teachers and education should be promoted in the whole society."[19]

In terms of teaching methods, the Chinese government has promoted the close integration of modern information technology with education and teaching, fully promoted the application of modern education and teaching methods to the teaching practice, and achieved good teaching effects.

In terms of the management of educational institutions, the Chinese government has operated the system of separation between the management, running, and assessment of schools, expand the decision-making powers of schools, improve inspection of and oversight over education, and strengthen social oversight over education. Meanwhile, the Chinese government has established a system of policies for management according to institution type and for the provision of differentiated support, and encourage non-governmental actors and investors to provide a diverse range of education services.

In terms of investment in education, the Chinese government has increased its investment in education, and relying on the rule of law from the central to the local level, ensured investment in education. The Chinese government has also improved its financial support system for education and students, achieving full coverage of financial support for students from financially disadvantaged families and enhancing the vitality of education development.

Xi Jinping pointed out: "To realize the Chinese Dream of national rejuvenation, the position and role of education cannot be neglected."[20] Running a modern education that people are satisfied with is an important aspect of paying attention to safeguarding and improving people's wellbeing in society building in China. Practice proved that since the 18th CPC National Congress, the Chinese government has made every effort to promote running a modern education that people are satisfied with, and on the basis of

---

19   Ibid.
20   Zhang Shuo, Put Ideological and Political Education throughout the Whole Teaching Process and Create a New Situation in the Development of China's Higher Education, *People's Daily*, December 9, 2016, p. 1.

adhering to the basic theories of Marxism on education and combined with the basic national conditions of Chinese education, realized the Chinese characteristics of China's education. On the basis of adhering to the basic principles of China's socialist education, the fine traditions of the Chinese education have been inherited, the outstanding educational achievements of other countries in the world have been drawn on, the distinctive characteristics of China's times. Running a modern education that people are satisfied with has safeguarded and improved the wellbeing of the broad masses of the people and provided a basic driving force for society building in China.

II. Advancing the construction of a healthy China

Pushing forward building a healthy China is a great social system project. Since the 18th CPC National Congress, the Central Committee of the Communist Party of China has elevated "Healthy China" to a national strategy and established the world's largest basic medical insurance network within a relatively short period of time. Paying much attention to the development of the cause of people's health, and Xi Jinping emphasized on the National Sanitation and Health Conference: "Health is a must for promoting well-rounded personal development, a prerequisite for economic and social development, a symbol of national prosperity and strength, and a common pursuit of all people." Therefore, health is the inevitable requirements for the philosophy of "putting the people at the center" upheld all the time by the Party and government, and an important symbol of people's happiness.

On May 10, 2017, jointly launched by Fengtai District Health and Planning Commission and Fengtai District Disease Prevention and Control Center in Beijing, the second walking movement "Meeting there for walking 10,000 steps" was carried out in Yuan Bo Park for the occupational group. The picture shows one scene of the brisk walk activity.

Health is an eternal pursuit of human development. Without health there is no happiness. To build a healthy China, Xi Jinping emphasized: "If we cannot ensure the people's health, we cannot achieve moderate prosperity in all respects. We should prioritize public health, popularizing a healthy lifestyle, improving health services and security, building a healthy environment, and developing health industries. We should quicken our pace in implementing the healthy China program, striving to ensure all-round people's health at all times. These are the requirements of good health in realizing the 'two centenary' goals and the Chinese Dream of national rejuvenation."[21] To push forward building a healthy China, the Chinese government has deepened the reform of the medical and health system, improved the universal medical insurance system, strengthened the basic public health care services, perfected the health care services system, ensured the safety of food and drugs, enhanced the maternal and child health care, and improved the level of people's health and welfare.

1. The reform of the medical and health system has been deepened

Since the 18th CPC National Congress, the government has coordinated and advanced the comprehensive reform of the medical insurance, medical services, public health, drug supply and supervision system, etc.. Xi Jinping pointed out: "We should adhere to sound public health principles, prioritizing community-level health work and driven by reform and innovations; focus on disease prevention; and develop both traditional Chinese medicine and Western medicine. We should incorporate health care into all our policies, and ensure the people contribute to the cause and share the benefits."[22] Therefore, in recent years, the Chinese government has coordinated medical services, medical insurance, and pharmaceutical reforms, promote the separation of medical care from pharmacy operations, and establish a sound basic healthcare system covering all citizens. It has executed comprehensive reform of all public hospitals to see that they are there to serve the public without having to make a profit, their operational costs are lowered, and markups on pharmaceuticals are gradually eliminated. It has carried out a pricing reform for medical services and improved public

---

21   Put People's Health in the Priority of Development Strategy and Strive to Fully Safeguard People's Health in All Respects, *People's Daily*, August 21, 2016, p. 1.
22   Ibid.

hospital compensation mechanisms. It has established modern hospital management systems, seen that public hospitals act as independent legal persons, and established staffing and remuneration systems suited to the particular characteristics of the healthcare industry.

The system of essential drugs has been improved, the reform of logistics systems for pharmaceuticals and consumables has been deepened, and medicine supply mechanisms have been improved. The Chinese government has encouraged the research and development of new drugs, and given precedence to newly developed drugs available on the market and drugs that have passed evaluations for consistency in adding to the catalogue of medicines covered by healthcare insurance. In terms of improving the quality of health services and encouraging the development of health care, Xi Jinping pointed out: "We should improve the quality and capacity of health care services which are accessible to all. We should balance the roles of government and market; the government should be operational in providing basic health care services, while the market should be dynamic in other health care areas".[23] As a result, the Chinese government has strengthened oversight over the healthcare industry across the board, improved the quality of health care, and ensured that health care is safe. It has created a better work environment for medical practitioners, and improved mechanisms for mediating disputes between them and patients to facilitate more amicable relations. Moreover, it has encouraged non-governmental actors to provide healthcare services and seen that non-profit private hospitals enjoy treatment equal to that of public hospitals.

2. The universal medical insurance system has been improved

The universal medical insurance system is the core content of the basic health care system of a healthy China. It is a matter of national prosperity, social stability and personal happiness. Since the 18th CPC National Congress, the Chinese government has accelerated the establishment and improvement of a multi-level health medical insurance system covering urban and rural residents on the basis of the initial realization of a universal basic medical insurance system. Xi Jinping emphasized: "We should maintain basic non-profit health care, continue to improve the health care

---

23   Ibid.

system, expand health care services and improve health care quality, so that the public can have equal access to systematic and consistent health care services from disease prevention through treatment, rehabilitation and health promotion."[24]

Actively advancing the improvement of the medical insurance system and policies. In terms of the concrete contents of refining the universal medical insurance system, the Chinese government has improved the mechanisms to ensure stable and sustainable funding for medical insurance and to adjust reimbursement rates for medical expenses, and improved payment policies for medical insurance premiums. It has fully implemented the major disease insurance scheme for rural and non-working urban residents, and improved the assistance systems for major or serious diseases and for emergency disease treatment, and lowered the treatment costs of major and chronic diseases. It has reformed medical insurance management and payment methods and kept medical expenses at a reasonable level, ensuring a sustainable balance of medical insurance funds. It has improved the personal account side of the basic medical insurance scheme and brought outpatient expenditures under unified management. By December 2020, the number of participants in the three basic medical insurance policies for urban employees and for rural and non-working urban residents and new rural cooperative medical care reached more than 1.33 billion reached more than 1.36 billion, and the urban and rural medical insurance participation rate stabilized at over 95%. In a relatively short period of time, the Chinese government has established the world's largest basic medical insurance network, and at the same time the level of insurance has been significantly improved.

The integration of urban and rural residents' medical insurance has been advanced. In recent years, the Chinese government has promoted the integration of the medical insurance policies for rural and non-working urban residents along with the management of insurance. It has promoted the integration of the basic medical care insurance of rural and non-working urban residents and new rural cooperative medical system, and established a unified basic medical insurance system for urban and rural residents. The Chinese government has advanced the reform of the health care system, the fair enjoyment of urban and rural residents' basic medical insurance rights and benefits, promoted social fairness and justice and improved people's

---

24 Ibid.

medical welfare. In accordance with the general idea of unifying systems, integrating policies, balancing levels, improving mechanisms and enhancing services, the Chinese government has strengthened the integration of urban and rural residents' medical insurance in terms of unified coverage, unified funding policy, unified protection treatment, unified medical insurance catalog, unified fixed-point management, and unified fund management, etc., and established an urban and rural residents' medical insurance system with fairer protection, more standardized management services, and more effective utilization of medical resources. The Chinese government has promoted and realized the "Three Medical Linkages" of medical care, medical insurance and medicine, and promoted and perfected the multi-level medical insurance system including basic insurance, major disease insurance, medical assistance, commercial health insurance, social charity, etc..

Efforts to enable medical bills incurred in any locality to be settled through basic medical insurance accounts have been sped up. In the recent

The health insurance system in Zhejiang Province was incorporated into the national medical settlement system and the nationwide network operation achieved. The picture shows the residents use social security cards to settle the medical fees at the smart medical multifunctional self-help machines in Yinzhou People's Hospital, Ningbo.

years, the Chinese government has achieved that a retiree living in a different province from that in which premium payments were made can settle inpatient expenditures where they were incurred, and encouraged commercial insurance agencies to participate in providing medical insurance. In addition, the Chinese government has promoted the merge of the maternity insurance into the basic medical insurance scheme, carried out pilot work on long-term care insurance and the integration of medical insurance and maternity insurance, and encouraged the development of supplementary medical insurance and commercial health insurance, explored and established long-term care insurance system, and carried out pilot projects of long-term care insurance. It has improved the medical malpractice insurance system, actively promoted the provincial-level coordination of workers' compensation, and steadily improved the level of social security benefits. In 2020, government subsidies for basic medical insurance for rural and non-working urban residents were increased by 30 RMB per person, per year, reaching no less than 550 RMB per person per year. Meanwhile, the individual insurance contributions have been increased, and the scope of the insurance for drug use have been expanded.

3. Basic public health services have been strengthened

Basic public health services are an important part of pushing forward the construction of a healthy China and an important work in deepening the reform of the medical and health system. During his study in Jiangsu, Xi Jinping pointed out emphatically: "If we cannot ensure people's health, we cannot achieve moderate prosperity in all respects. Medical and health services directly affect people's physical health. We should shift the focus of health care work, decentralize medical resources, equalize basic public services in urban and rural areas, and provide the safe and effective public health care and basic medical services for people so that people's problem of inadequate and overly expensive medical services can be solved." Since the 18th CPC National Congress, the Chinese government has strengthened basic public health services.

First, the national basic public health services and major public health services have been improved, the, efficiency and equalization level of services have been increased and increased the basic public health service capacity has been raised. On October 23, 2012, when Xi Jinping met with

President of the French Alain Meniere's Foundation, he said: "The Chinese government attaches foremost importance to the development of health care, emphasizing the importance of ensuring people's health and life safety. China will continue to push forward the reform and development of the medical and health care undertakings, initially establish the basic medical and health system covering urban and rural residents, improve the basic medical insurance system, perfect the public health and medical services system, and further raise the level of health of the masses."

Secondly, the comprehensive prevention and control of major diseases such as maternal and child health, public health, chronic diseases, infectious diseases and endemic diseases and the prevention and control of occupational hazards have been strengthened. On November 25, 2015, at the Commendation Conference for Ebola Epidemic Prevention and Control, Xi Jinping emphasized: "We should always put health and safety of the people in the first place, and effectively work on infectious disease

On December 1, 2015, the 28ᵗʰ World AIDS Day, volunteers stick red ribbons symbol of AIDS prevention on a billboard in support of a campus HIV/AIDS awareness event at Northwest University in Xi'an, Shaanxi province.

prevention and strengthen the quick response to public health emergency." In recent years, the Chinese government has enhanced the capacity of improving maternal and child health, public health, cancer prevention, mental illness control and pediatrics. The comprehensive prevention and control strategy of chronic diseases was established, which effectively scales up against the chronic diseases such as cardio-cerebrovascular disease, diabetes mellitus, malignant tumor and respiratory diseases. More efforts are spent on the prevention and control of major infectious diseases, the Hepatitis B infection rate of entire population has been reduced, the incidence of tuberculosis has reached to 58/100,000, the schistosomiasis was basically eliminated, and the risk of malaria and leprosy was reduced to nearly zero. The prevention and control work for key endemic diseases has achieved important steps. The survey and prevention of occupational diseases were carried out. The port health and quarantine capacity has been improved to prevent the importation of major infectious diseases. About AIDS prevention and treatment, Xi Jinping is particularly concerned, and emphasized: "The fight against AIDS is a complex medical issue, also an urgent welfare issue and a social issue. It demands all people's participation, full input, and all-round prevention. From the perspective of personal health, family happiness and social harmony, we should deal with the AIDS prevention and control work."[25] In recent years, the Chinese government has increased the free supply of special drugs for AIDS prevention and treatment and the AIDS epidemic has been controlled at a low epidemic level.

Thirdly, patriotic cleaning campaigns and efforts to improve the level of urban and rural health and beauty have been stepped up. Xi Jinping pointed out: "We should carry forward the tradition of patriotic cleaning campaign, continue with the urban and rural clean environment campaigns, increase efforts in improving rural living conditions and build a healthy and livable environment."[26] In recent years, the Chinese government has deeply carried out patriotic cleaning campaigns and the construction of health and livable cities and towns. Education on health awareness for the whole population have been strengthened, the national nutrition program and mental health services have been strengthened. A wide range of health promotion activities

25   Li Bin, The Whole Society Must Illuminate Their Life with Love-Xi Jinping in Beijing to Participate in the Related Activities at World AIDS Day, *People's Daily*, December 1, 2012, p. 1.
26   Put People's Health in the Priority of Development Strategy and Strive to Fully Safeguard People's Health in All Respects, *People's Daily*, August 21, 2016, p. 1.

have been launched, a healthy lifestyle has been advocated, a major push to prohibit smoking in public places has been made and the health-related literacy of the entire population has been raised. Meanwhile, the Chinese government has also pushed forward environmental sanitation and clean-up campaigns in towns and cities, increased the vigor of the rural living environment governance, promoted the optimization of urban and rural environments, making the sky bluer, mountains greener and water clearer, and remarkable results have been made in the construction of beautiful cities and towns.

4. The medical services system has been perfected

Since the 19th CPC National Congress, the Chinese government has perfected the medical services system. Xi Jinping pointed out: "We should advocate a healthy lifestyle, promote the idea of all-round wellness, shift the focus from treating ailments to health care, improve health care education system, enhance the health awareness of the public and integrate fitness and health care across the country. We should increase efforts in the basic research of mental health, promote popular understanding of mental health and mental illness and regulate psychotherapy, psychological counseling and other mental health services."[27] Therefore, the Chinese government has optimized the structure of medical institutions, moved forward the innovation on functional integration and service mode, strengthened the division and collaboration between professional public health institutions, primary medical and health institutions and hospitals, perfected the system of medical service with the linkage between top and bottom, improved the basic medical service mode, enhanced the capacity of general practitioners (family doctors), pushed forward the electronic health recording and implemented the family doctor contracted pattern.

The system of grading diagnosis and treatment has been established comprehensively. To improve primary medical services, the Chinese government has advanced the service network, operation mechanism and incentive mechanism, implemented the differential insurance payment and price policy, formed a scientific and reasonable health and medical order, and generally achieved the primary diagnosis at community level, the

---

27 Ibid.

two-way referral, the linkage between the upper and community level, and the corresponding treatment towards acute or chronic diseases.

Emphasis has been placed on improving the development of medical and health teams. We have implemented the National Health personnel Security Project and a plan for general practitioners, pediatric doctors to be trained and employed, and improved the resident doctor training system. We also have promoted the working environment and salary system of medical staff and improved the doctor's multi-sited licensed system. In 2020, there are 2.92 physicians and physician assistants per 1000 population, 3.56 registered nurses per 1,000 population, 2.89 general practitioners per 10,000 population and 6.97 number of public health workers per 10,000 population. At the same time, the medical resources have been weighted towards the central and western regions, the grassroots and rural areas. The Chinese government has made all-round implementation of the clinical pathway, improved health information services, enhanced large-scale data application capabilities, and developed telemedical and smart medical treatments.

5. Food and drug safety has been ensured

Since the 18th CPC National Congress, the Chinese government has ensured food and drug safety. Xi Jinping pointed out: "We should strengthen food and drug safety regulation effectively, should accelerate the establishment of a scientific and perfect food and drug safety management system with the most stringent standards, the most strict supervision, the most severe punishment and the most serious accountability, should adhere to the balance between production and management and should strictly check every line from the farmland to the table, from the laboratory to the hospital."[28]

First, in terms of food, the Chinese government has implemented the food safety strategy and strengthened the monitoring and evaluation of food safety. Xi Jinping pointed out: "We should improve the quality and safety of agricultural produces, make more efforts to ensure the quality and safety of agricultural produces and enhance the quality and safety supervision system of agricultural produces. We should also put the quality and safety of food as a key factor in agricultural transformation and adjustment

---

28   Firmly Uphold the Concept of Effective Implementation of Security Development and Protect People's Lives and Property, *People's Daily*, May 31, 2015, p. 1.

On December 1, 2015, the 28ᵗʰ World AIDS Day, volunteers stick red ribbons symbol of AIDS prevention on a billboard in support of a campus HIV/AIDS awareness event at Northwest University in Xi'an, Shaanxi province.

period, expecting people to eat safely and confidently."[29] In recent years, the Chinese government has improve food safety laws and regulations, raise food safety standards, focus greater effort on addressing food safety problems at the source, require all food enterprises to assume responsibility for food safety, exercise grid-based oversight, increase the frequency of inspections and the coverage of sample-based monitoring, and achieve product traceability throughout the whole production chain. The model food safety cities have been developed. Xi Jinping emphasized: "We should enforce food safety laws, improve the food safety system and strengthen food safety supervision from farmland to the dining table."[30]

Second, in terms of drugs, the Chinese government has deepened reform of the evaluation and approval system for pharmaceuticals and medical appliances and explore reform of evaluation institutions based on an independent corporate governance model.

---

29   Ibid.
30   Put People's Health in the Priority of Development Strategy and Strive to Fully Safeguard People's Health in All Respects, *People's Daily*, August 21, 2016, p. 1.

Third, in terms of the construction of a food and drug supervision system, the Chinese government has accelerated improvements to the food supervision system and built a sound governance system for food and medicine safety that is thorough, efficient, and based on co-governance by social actors. Xi Jinping pointed out: "Food and drug safety is related to everyone's physical health and life safety. Therefore, with the most stringent standards, the strictest supervision, the most severe punishment, the most serious accountability, we should ensure people's tongue safety. Also, we should speed up the establishment of relevant safety standards, accelerate the construction of a scientific and better food and drug safety management system, strive to make the quality of food and drugs safe, stable and controlled and the security level has been significantly improved."[31] The government has stepped up food and medicine safety governance in rural areas and improve oversight over online sales of food and medicine. Meanwhile, the Chinese government has conduct tighter oversight over imported food and medicine. The Chinese government has enabled broad masses of people eat and use drugs at ease by strengthening the food and drug safety management.

6. The level of maternal and child health care has been improved

Since the 18th CPC National Congress, the Chinese government has improved maternal and child health care to comprehensively push forward the Healthy China Initiative. Xi Jinping emphasized: "We should carry out the disease prevention policy, raising the public's awareness to prevent and control epidemics and striving to provide the people with life-cycle health care services. We should pay attention to the prevention and control of major diseases, improving related strategies to minimize the number of patients. We should attach importance to the health of children and adolescents, improving health care in kindergartens, primary and secondary schools; increasing the health care publicity to enhance students' awareness of disease prevention, and providing nutritious meals to young students in poverty-stricken areas to ensure their health growth. We should pay attention to the health of special groups, protecting women's and children's health; providing consistent health management services and medical services to

---

31   The Party Literature Research Office of the CPC Central Committee, *Excerpts from Xi Jinping's Treatises on Building a Moderately Prosperous Society in All Respects*, Central Party Literature Press, 2016, p. 151.

senior citizens; striving to achieve the goal of providing rehabilitation services to every disabled person; caring about the health of migrant population; and implementing health care related poverty relief projects."[32] The government has fully implemented the system of subsidy for birth giving at hospital to provide free basic maternal health care services in the entire pregnancy process, strengthened the birth defects prevention and control, and established a free service system for birth defects prevention covering all phases through pre-pregnancy, pregnancy and new birth for urban and rural residents.

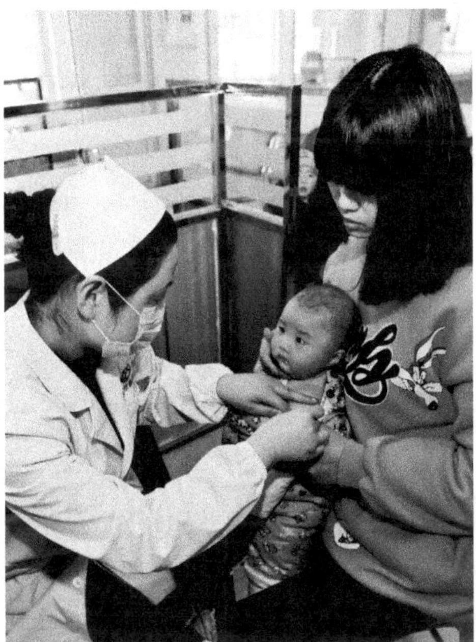

On March 18, 2015, Mingguang Disease Prevention and Control Center in Anhui Province launched a campaign for free measles vaccination and the vaccine leak finding and replanting to work well on the prevention and control of measles. A child is vaccinated against measles free of charge.

---

32 Put People's Health in the Priority of Development Strategy and Strive to Fully Safeguard People's Health in All Respects, *People's Daily*, August 21, 2016, p. 1.

We have comprehensively enhanced maternal and child health service capacity, strengthened the prevention and treatment of key diseases of women and children, improved the screening rate of common diseases and early diagnosis for women, enforced the prevention and treatment of childhood diseases and injuries, fully implemented child nutrition improvement and neonatal screening programs in impoverished areas. With the continuous improvement of Chinese people's living standard, their health has been significantly improved. China's health care system has been guided by Xi Jinping's Thought on Socialism with Chinese Characteristics for a New Era during the period of 13th Five-Year Plan. The health care sector has resolutely carried out the decisions and deployments of the CPC Central Committee and the State Council in promoting the healthy China project, with new progress in advancing the medical and health care undertakings, new achievements in deepening the reform of the health. Such health care system has withstood the test of the COVID-19 epidemic. From 2015 to 2019, the average life expectancy of Chinese residents increased from 76.34 years to 77.3 years, the main health indicators were generally better than the average level of middle and high-income countries, and the proportion of personal health expenditure in total health expenditure decreased to 28.4%, laying a solid health basis for building a moderately prosperous society in all respects.

7. The COVID-19 epidemic has been prevailed over

The year of 2020 promises to be one of the most extraordinary years in history because of the COVID-19 epidemic that started in late 2019. COVID-19 is the most serious epidemic the world has seen in a hundred years. It is the fastest spreading, most infectious, and hardest to control public health emergency that China has encountered since 1949. The outbreak of COVID-19 has had a great impact on the people around the world, including the Chinese people. The CPC Central Committee has led the Chinese people in fighting a tenacious battle against COVID-19, we worked with unity and solidarity, and finally prevailed over COVID-19 epidemic.

In the course of the fight against the COVID-19, General Secretary Xi Jinping has personally commanded, planned the response, overseen the general situation and acted decisively, pointing the way forward in the fight against the epidemic. In the face of the unexpected COVID-19 situation, the CPC Central Committee took decisive decisions and adopted "extraordinary measures" to tackle the epidemic, urging all citizens to help fight and win the battle against the epidemic by mobilizing all resources, and blocking the spread of the virus.

The CPC Central Committee with Comrade Xi as the core put the health and lives of Chinese people in the first place, and demonstrated collective and unified leadership in the first instance. The Political Bureau and Standing Committee of the CPC Central Committee have convened 21 meetings to study the situation, and mobilized all sectors of Chinese society and all regions across the country to engage in a nationwide battle. It has been a work with confidence and unity, and in a scientific and targeted work style. The general goal was to resolutely stop the outbreak, and resolutely win the battle against COVID-19. Well planned arrangements were made to give a helping hand to Wuhan city and the whole Hubei province, and effective strategies which suited to the evolving situation was implemented.

With a swift response, we set up a central leading group to fight against the COVID-19, sent a central command group to the Hubei province, and established an inter-provincial task force under the leadership of State Council. We emphasized early detection, early reporting, early quarantine, and early treatment, and concentrated resources, experts and facilities to treat severe cases. Great efforts were made to increase the admission rate and cure rate, thus greatly reduced the infection rate and the fatality rate.

In the process of strenuous epidemic prevention and control and having all patients cured, we did everything we could to treat infected individuals, leaving no stones unturned, and leaving no one behind. It has drawn on a combination of Chinese and Western medicine, and the state bore all the treatment related expenses, so that it was able to improve the cure rate and reduce the fatality rate to the fullest extent. There has been a focus on research and development in conjunction with clinical treatment and prevention and control protocols. We developed a testing kit at the earliest possible time, and accelerated the research and development of effective medicines and vaccines, giving full play to science and technology in national epidemic prevention and control. Besides, we rapidly put in place a nationwide information sharing mechanism and released relevant information in a factual and transparent way.

While strengthening the national epidemic prevention and control, we constantly think about the safety and health of Chinese citizens abroad, and tried all means to secure their health in life and study. We sent health kits to them, and helped those in need who are living and working abroad to return to China in an orderly fashion. In accordance with the changing situation, we shifted the focus to preventing inbound cases and resurgence of domestic COVID-19 cases, replacing extraordinary emergency response with normalized regular control, so that it could detect cases and handle them promptly, control outbreaks in a calibrated fashion, and treated cases in an effective way.

Under the leadership CPC Central Committee with Xi Jinping at the core, governments and party committees at all levels, official departments and institutions across the country responded to the call of duty. Villages, communities, enterprises, health institutions, research institutes, schools, universities and military barracks all played their due role under the strong leadership of the CPC central committee. The whole nation took unified orders, made all-round arrangements, and adopted multi-pronged measures. Thus, we were able to effectively prevent the large-scale spread, blunt the trajectory of the virus to the largest extent possible, and protected people's lives and health.

China has achieved a great victory in containing the spread of the virus, providing rich experience for the Chinese people, and the people around the world. Our victory over the virus is attributable to the strong leadership of the CPC Central Committee with Xi Jinping at the core. The CPC Central Committee and Xi Jinping always give top priority to people's safety and health, make decisive decisions, give unified orders, make all-round arrangements, and thus ensured the success in combatting the COVID-19 epidemic. The systemic strength of socialism with Chinese characteristics and fully released governance effectiveness constituted the strong guarantee for collectively overcoming difficulties and fighting the COVID-19 epidemic. Adhering to the principles of serving the people and relying on the people constitutes the source of power that pushed us forward through all types of hardship to prevail over the epidemic. The great spirit forged during the fight against COVID-19 is a powerful engine for taking the bull by the horn and fighting until the end. We hold the concept of a community with a shared future for mankind and takes our share of responsibility in solidarity and cooperation, which points out the right path to the final victory over the coronavirus. Enhancing its comprehensive strength in development and better respond to possible risks and challenges enable us to take firm steps towards the future.

In this deadly battle against the serious epidemic, the Chinese people and Chinese nation have shown the heroic courage to fight and to win, and the great anti-epidemic spirit of cherishing life, coming together as one, risking one's own life to help others, respect for science, and caring for each other. The great victory of this battle against COVID-19 has produced a notable result: China's character, strength and sense of responsibility have been shown throughout the struggle. The major strategic gains accomplished in the battle against COVID-19 have fully testified to the great strengths of the CPC leadership and our country's socialist system, fully testified to the great strength and resilience of the Chinese people and the Chinese nation, fully testified to the profound foundation of the Chinese civilization. They have fully demonstrated the strong sense of responsibility of China as a major responsible country, they have greatly strengthened the confidence, pride, unity, and solidarity of the whole party and all ethnic groups of the country. They will inspire the Chinese people to overcome all obstacles and forge ahead in their new journey in a new era.

The CPC Central Committee has protected people's health and safety by leading people to overcome the COVID-19 epidemic. It's a striking contrast to Western countries' weak response to the pandemic. During the process of China's epidemic prevention and control, a vast number of medical personnel have been in the forefront, and a vast number of party members and cadres have worked around the clock. The voices of party members and cadres can be heard at any time. The basic fact of victory over COVID-19 once again proves that it is absolutely right to adhere to the leadership of the CPC Central Committee in China. China must uphold the leadership of the Communist Party of China and take the road of socialism with Chinese characteristics.

Chapter Three

Safeguarding and Improving People's Wellbeing

Safeguarding and improving people's wellbeing can give full play to the important role of benefiting people's wellbeing, warming people's hearts, alleviating people's worries, and gathering people's strength. In early February 2016, when Xi Jinping went to Jiangxi to visit and condole the cadres and masses, he pointed out: "There is no ending but continuous starting point in safeguarding and improving people's wellbeing. We should take more targeted, more extensive, more direct and more effective measures to really help the masses solve their problems, to increase their welfare and let them enjoy fairness. We should take the reality into consideration, concentrate our efforts on the construction of inclusive, basic and bottom-line people's wellbeing, constantly improve the ability of joint construction and the sharing level of public services, weave a tight and firm wellbeing 'safety net' to help those most in need, eliminate hidden dangers, and ensure that the masses live and work in peace and contentment and the society is stable and orderly". Since the 18th CPC National Congress, the Chinese government has pushed forward priority development of social employment, increased the residents' income in a shared development, perfected the social security system in the urban and rural areas, and improved the people's living standards in all respects. By safeguarding and improving people's wellbeing, China has achieved that the fruits of reform and development are shared by all, effectively enhancing the people's sense of fulfillment and improving their welfare on all fronts.

I.   Pushing forward giving priority to the development of social employment

The 18th CPC National Congress pointed out: "Employment is pivotal to people's wellbeing". Employment is closely related to the daily life of the people. One of the key points of society building is that the people live and work in peace and contentment which is also the basic supportive project to maintain social peace and stability and ensure people's happiness. Xi Jinping pointed out: "We will focus our efforts on employment work. Employment is pivotal to people's wellbeing. We should adhere to the strategy prioritizing employment, implement a more active employment policy, create more jobs, make efforts to solve structural employment problems, encourage entrepreneurship to boost employment, and achieve fuller and high-quality employment."[1] The 19th CPC National Congress pointed out: "Employment is pivotal to people's wellbeing. We must give high priority to employment and pursue a proactive employment policy, striving to achieve fuller employment and create better quality jobs". The Chinese government has given priority to promoting employment, gradually implemented the strategy prioritizing employment, and achieved higher-quality employment.

1. Higher-quality employment has been achieved

Since the 18th CPC National Congress, the Chinese government has given priority to promoting fuller employment and achieving high quality employment in the economic and social development and placed them in a prominent position. Xi Jinping pointed out: "Employment is affecting the lives of millions of households, and a job can help to earn income and improve living standards. Employment is also the basic condition for workers to integrate into society, realize their own self-fulfillments and share the fruits of economic and social development. Only by achieving comparatively full employment, can we build a prosperous society in all respects and make people have a real sense of fulfillment."[2] To achieve full employment, the Chinese government has focused on the employment classification policy, increased the labor participation rate, and steadily expanded the urban employment scale. The high-quality employment policy implemented by the

---

1   *A Series of Important Speeches by General Secretary Xi Jinping* (2016 ed.), compiled by the Publicity Department of the CPC Central Committee, People's Press, 2016, p. 216.
2   Bai Tianliang, Let the People Obtain More Reliable Wellbeing Security (Concepts of the 13th Five-Year Plan), *People's Daily*, April 16, 2016, p. 6.

To promote the public awareness for business start-ups and innovations, on February 15, 2017, the Xi'an Municipal Trade Union and the City Bureau jointly held a large-scale job fair titled Spring Movement of the Employment Assistance Month in 2017, in the Qujiang International Convention and Exhibition Center in order to promote the prioritized employment strategy and carry out Xian's employment and entrepreneurship preferential policy through practical actions.

Chinese government not only attaches importance to the continuous expansion of the employment scale in the whole society, but also pays attention to the steady improvement of employment quality and reinforce the continuity and stability of employment. To achieve high-quality employment, the Chinese government has formulated and implemented the employment promotion and the pioneering plan for undergraduates, has set up the platform for innovation and entrepreneurship, has improved the employment incentive policy of national undergraduates' self-employment and community-based independent entrepreneurship. To promote the full employment of all kinds of people in the society, the Chinese government, through policy guidance, has promoted the shift of rural surplus labors and the returning workers to start up their businesses at home. It has also strengthened the support for the flexible employment and new forms of employment, and also promoted workers' self-employment. it has done a good job in the employment and resettlement of retired military personnel.

The Chinese government has also strengthened employment security and the unemployment assistance, has carried on the real-name dynamic management and the targeted help for those people who have difficulties in getting jobs, completed the supporting work for "zero employment" families, has increased the support for re-employment, has improved the working conditions, standardized the labor and employment-service system, implemented the annual paid vacation system for the working staff. In addition, the Chinese government has strengthened legal aid and employment protection, strictly prohibited all forms of discrimination in employment, institutionalized the employment intermediary service, improved the coordination mechanism of labor relations, strengthened the labor security supervision and dispute mediation arbitration, protected the lawful rights and interests of the employees, guaranteed the rights and interests of the irregular employees, fully addressed the issue of wage arrears for peasant workers, established the harmonious labor relations, and promoted the stable and orderly development of society. Overall, China's employment situation remains stable in general. According to the National Bureau of Statistics of China, from January to November 2020, 10.99 million new urban jobs were created, accounting for 122.1% of the annual target. In November, China's urban unemployment rate was 5.2%, 0.1% lower than that in October, falling for four consecutive months; among them, the unemployment rate of the 25-59-year-old population was 4.7%, 0.1% lower. The unemployment rate in 31 big cities was 5.2%, down 0.1 percentage point from October. The practice of Linyi City, Shandong Province, a famous old revolutionary base in China, to achieve higher-quality employment is highly typical.

Since the 18th CPC National Congress, to achieve a higher-quality employment, the Linyi government has creatively launched the "Go Out", "Stay On", "Create" campaigns, to help push the rural labor force out to achieve a higher-quality employment.

Organizing "Go Out" is to open up a new world of employment for Yimeng people. In order to enable more peasants to find good jobs and obtain good income, Linyi has created a "three-pronged" working mode of training, employment and rights protection. When the "matchmaker" acts as a bridge, when the "mother's family" solves problems, and when the "mother-in-law's family" provides follow-up services, more than 2 million rural labor forces have realized an orderly transfer, and the labor income accounts for more than 50% of the per capita net income of peasants. The legitimate rights and interests of labor exporters have been safeguarded with the establishment of 103 labor services agencies stationed abroad and more than 10 mobile party organizations; the tracking and management service for labor exporters have been strengthened, and the labor trademark "Yimeng Star" has been branded and a large number of outstanding representatives of migrant workers and management services agencies stationed abroad with "home" brand emerged.

Pushing forward "Stay On" is to give priority to meet the new needs of local enterprises' development. In recent years, in view of the rapid development of county and town economy and the rapid growth of employment demand, Linyi City has timely changed its work ideas, and made more rural labor force obtain employment in their home town by strengthening skill training, building a supply-demand bridge and strengthening public services. We have been vigorously promoting the construction of a strong human resources city, implementing projects such as "one million rural labourers' employment skills and transfer training", "golden blue-collar" training and government purchase of training results, deepening joint school-enterprise education, implementing order-based and targeted training, and training about 250,000 people of all kinds every year. The training programme has trained about 250,000 people each year, and over 90% of them have been employed in their local areas.

Guiding "Create" is to open up new ways of employment driven by entrepreneurship. Linyi has taken the opportunity to create provincial-level entrepreneurial cities in Lanshan District and Linshu County, starting with improving support policies such as entrepreneurial subsidies, entrepreneurial training and small guaranteed loans, and improving the "three-pronged" working mechanism of policy support, entrepreneurial training and entrepreneurial services to provide entrepreneurs with "one-stop" and "one-station" services such as financing guarantee, entrepreneurial training, information and consultation, entrepreneurial guidance, project promotion, technical support and social security. Two demonstration parks for university students' entrepreneurship have been established at the municipal level, and one entrepreneurship service center integrating training, employment, incubation and other functions has been established in each county.[3]

---

3   Sheng Li, "Going Out", "Stay on" and "Create"–Linyi Government Pushing the Rural Labor Force to Achieve Higher-quality Employment, *Shandong Human Resources and Social Security*, 2013(9).

2. The capacity of public employment services has been raised

The public employment and business startup need a favorable social environment, which requires the government to lead various forces in society to participate in the formation and promotion of the good social environment. Thus, the Chinese government has constantly improved its own capacity of serving the public employment and innovations, comprehensively implemented various measures, mobilized the strength of all walks of life, and jointly create a good social environment for public employment and entrepreneurship. As Xi Jinping has pointed out: "The party and the government should issue more active employment policies, create more job vacancies, improve the employment environment, enhance the employment quality, and constantly increase the labor remuneration, especially the front-line workers. We should establish and improve Party and government-led mechanism of safeguarding people's rights and interests, focus on the problems of labor and employment, train people for better skills, income distribution, social security, safety and health and so on, pay attention to the frontline workers, migrant workers, workers with difficulties and other disadvantaged groups, improve the mechanism, eliminate obstacles to the participation and growth of workers, obstacles to sharing development results, and strive to enable workers to achieve decent employment and all-round development. We should steadily work for the people, warm-heartedly in real sense.

We should put people's safety and well-being first, timely help them, relieve them from difficulties, offer down-to-earth solution to the problems which people are most concerned about, and to the practical problems which are the most difficult, most anxious and the most urgent."[4]

Since the 18th CPC National Congress, the Chinese government has advanced the employment and entrepreneurship service system and implemented the lifelong vocational skills training system. The government has offered free vocational training for children from poor families, early secondary school graduates, migrant workers, unemployed and displaced workers, former military personnel and disabled persons. It has enhanced the social policy of professional title evaluation and technical grading of high-skilled personnel, has improved the employment and unemployment

---

4   Xi Jinping, *Speech on the Conference in Celebration of the May 1ˢᵗ Labor Day and and Cherishing the Honor of National Model Workers and Advanced Workers*, People's Press, 2015, pp. 7-8.

statistics index system, advanced the unemployment monitoring and early warning mechanism, timely released the urban survey of unemployment data, strengthened monitoring and response level of part of the region, industry scale unemployment. At the same time, the government has improved the informatization level of the public employment and entrepreneurship service and promoted the openness and sharing of all kinds of employment information. Through these measures, the Chinese government has greatly improved the capacity of the public employment service, promoted China's employment quality, enlarged China's employment scale, realized the full employment of Chinese society, improved the people's living standard and happiness index, and pushed forward the harmonious and stable development of the society.

3. The employment and entrepreneurship of college graduates has been promoted

The employment of college graduates is an important aspect of employment work in society building. To promote the successful employment of college graduates effectively is of great practical significance to ensure full employment in society. In recent years, the task of Chinese college graduates' employment is arduous, and the pressure is enormous. There were about 8 million 740 thousand graduated students in 2020, accounting for more than half of the new urban labor force. Because of the epidemic and the economic downturn, the task of employment has been very heavy. Since the 18th CPC National Congress, Chinese government has firmly put the employment of college graduates in the first place, taken new measures to new situations, done research and formulated new policies, and by all means promoted graduates' employment and entrepreneurship.

The Chinese government has improved and implemented the employment and entrepreneurship support policies for college graduates, improved the service guarantee mechanism, encouraged and guided the graduates to work at the grassroots level and broadened the employment channels for college graduates. Xi Jinping pointed out: "Youth is the hope of the country and the nation, innovation is the soul of social progress and entrepreneurship is an important access to promote economic and social development and improve people's wellbeing. Young students are imaginative and creative, and they are the active force of innovative entrepreneurship. We expect that a considerable number of young students integrate pursues of their own life into the national development and progress and the people's great practice, work hard, act down-to-earth, forge ahead, display talent in the innovation of entrepreneurship, and serve the society."[5] The Chinese government has improved the policy of for promoting the employment of college graduates and for guiding them in starting their own businesses in the central and western regions and at the grassroots level. To this end, the Chinese government has implemented policy-focused national key projects to promote employment and entrepreneurship, such as the "Go West Plan", "Three Assists, One Help", "Pre-recruitment of College Graduates for Military Service", "Tuition Free Normal College Students", "Special Recruitment Plan for Rural Teachers", "College Students Serve the Village", etc., and has achieved remarkable results in promoting multi-channel employment and entrepreneurship for the majority of college graduates.

The Chinese government has deeply implemented the employment and entrepreneurship promotion program for college graduates. To promote the employment of college graduates, the Chinese government and the society have created a good social environment for the employment and entrepreneurship of college graduates. As Xi Jinping emphasized: "The whole society should pay attention to and support youth for innovation and entrepreneurship, provide more favorable conditions and build a broader stage, so that the vast number of young people in the innovation and entrepreneurship can be shinning more brilliantly."[6] The Chinese government has formulated the feasible and preferential policy for employment and entrepreneurship, actively encouraged college graduates to start their own businesses, and tolerantly allowed them to fail. To promote the employment and entrepreneurship of college graduates, under the guidance of the Chinese government, the colleges and universities carried out five initiatives, such as capacity promotion, entrepreneurship guidance, employment support, protection of rights and interests, and campus targeted service. For graduates with difficulties in finding a job, they have also offered the special help with "One Person, One Policy" program to promote employment and entrepreneurship for more college graduates. The Chinese government has

---

5   A Congratulatory Letter from Xi Jinping to the Organizing Committee of the 2013 Global Entrepreneurship Week, *People's Daily*, November 9, 2013, p. 1.
6   Ibid.

also stepped up its efforts to ensure fair employment and entrepreneurial opportunities and created an objective and fair employment and entrepreneurial social environment. In addition, the Chinese government has provided college graduates with legal aid and legal protection through the rule of law for their employment and entrepreneurship, wiping off the worries of graduates about employment and entrepreneurship, and basically achieved the higher-quality employment of college graduates.

4. A fair employment environment has been created

A fair employment environment basically guarantees the full employment of the society. Since the 18ᵗʰ CPC National Congress, the Chinese government has vigorously created a fair employment environment, set up a good platform for employment, and gradually pushed forward full employment and higher-quality employment in the society. To promote employment by law and to tackle the employment problem with the rule of law is an important feature of China's employment policy since the 18ᵗʰ CPC National Congress. In April 2015, on the Fourteenth Session of the Standing Committee of the 12ᵗʰ National People's Congress, the *Employment Promotion Law of the People's Republic of China* was amended, which has played a crucial role in promoting employment, making progress in economic development, expanding employment, and achieving social harmony and stability. The Chinese government has actively implemented the *Employment Promotion Law of the People's Republic of China* in accordance with the law, with the promotion of various school-age youth employment, rural labor transfer employment, re-employment of personnel with difficulties and other work, increased the support on diverse types of self-employments, effectively prevented and eliminated employment discrimination, to create a fair employment and entrepreneurial environment in the whole society. At the same time, the Chinese government has also vigorously implemented a more active employment and entrepreneurship policy, mobilized the whole society to participate in the work of employment and entrepreneurship, and effectively created a more relaxed and better social environment conducive to employment and entrepreneurship.

Promoting the creation of equal opportunities in the employment environment. Through the recruitment by exams, according to the principle of information openness, process openness and result openness, the open recruitment system of public institutions has been improved and implemented, and the classified and grading public recruitment system has been carried out in the state-owned enterprises, which has promoted the reform of personnel system, expanded employment channels and created a fair employment environment. In the aspect of equal employment opportunities and fair employment environment, Shanxi Province steps in the forefront of the country.

Measure issued by the Shanxi Province: The Province's central, provincial, municipal and county state-owned enterprises must publish recruitment information on the designated public platform to ensure that the majority of job-seekers are informed in a timely manner, creating fair employment environment.

According to Measures on Public Released State-owned Enterprises Recruitment Information issued by Human Resources and Social Security Bureau of the Shanxi Province, the recruitment information of national and provincial state-owned enterprises in Shanxi Province should be published in the provincial public employment and talent service network and the employment network of college graduates; the city and county state-owned enterprises' recruitment information should be in the city and county public employment and talent service network, and other network platforms specified by the City and County Human Resources and Social Security Bureau.

The measures also require that the recruitment information issued by the state-owned enterprises should conform to the relevant laws, regulations and policies of the state and the province and ensure it's true and effective. The recruitment information should be released free of charge on the designated platform after examined by the local public employment service agencies. The public employment service agencies which have reviewed the recruitment information, will report the recruitment information on the designated platform within two days after the review is completed. In addition, the social security departments above the county level should strengthen the guidance and supervision of the state-owned enterprise recruitment information release system and create a fair employment environment.[7]

---

7   Zhou Yajun, The Recruitment Information of State-owned Enterprises in Shanxi Province Should Be Open to Public, *People's Daily*, July 9, 2013, p. 4.

The employment of young people with emphasis on college graduates has been vigorously promoted and the employment of rural migrant labor force, urban workers in difficulty, former military personnel and other employment placement work has been strengthened. Policies to encourage independent entrepreneurship, such as granting microcredits and financial subsidies have been perfected and implemented. The development of the service sector, labor-intensive enterprises, SMEs and innovative technology enterprises have been supported and protected and more jobs have been created. The tax and fee relief policy has been improved and the improvement of the subsidy policies for public-interest jobs, job training, social insurance and skill identification have been promoted.

The government has focused on helping migrant workers to achieve employment or entrepreneurship and created a fair employment environment. According to statistics, in more than 660 large and medium-sized cities in China, migrant workers amount to about 140 million people. Since the 18th CPC National Congress, in order to help migrant workers to achieve employment or entrepreneurship as soon as possible, the Ministry of Human Resources and Social Security of the PRC has vigorously carried out the "Spring Breeze Action" every year around the Spring Festival. The main contents of the "Spring Breeze Action" are to provide employment opportunities for migrant workers who go to cities for work, protect their legimate rights and interests, and rectify labor force intermediary institutions. The concrete measures of the "Spring Breeze Action" include strengthening employment services, deploying large-scale vocational training for migrant workers, stabilizing employment positions for migrant workers on the job, encouraging migrant workers to return to their hometowns to start their own businesses, promoting employment driven by entrepreneurship, deploying special actions to clean up and rectify the human resources market and protecting the legimate rights and interests of migrant workers. The "Spring Breeze Action" let many migrant workers who go to cities for work feel bathing in the spring breeze and feel ease under a "blue sky". In conjunction with the "Spring Breeze Action" and in combination with the traits of migrant workers' work and life, the Employment Promotion Department of the Ministry of Human Resources and Social Security plans and issues "Playing Cards with Information on Working in Cities" every spring. "Playing Cards with Information on Working in Cities" are an important publicity item in the "Spring Breeze Action". They have been continuously printed and issued for many years, achieved obvious publicity and educational results, effectively pushed forward the Chinese government's employment and entrepreneurship policies, effectively promoted migrant workers to enter the city for employment, and effectively helped migrant workers to return to their hometowns for business. The Chinese government's initiatives such as the "Spring Breeze Action" and the "Playing Cards with Information on Working in Cities" have effectively promoted social employment as a priority, promoted the achievement of full employment with high quality, and helped migrant workers in cities to find employment or return to their hometowns to start their own businesses.

II. Increasing the residents' income in a shared development

The income distribution system is a basic system in the framework of the socialist system with Chinese characteristics, and it is a fundamental and basic system in the development of China's economic society and an important cornerstone of the socialist market economy system. The income distribution system is directly related to the people's income and the vital interests. *Decision of the CPC Central Committee on Some Major Issues Concerning Comprehensively Deepening the Reform* points out: "A reasonable and orderly pattern of income distribution should be created." That is, a new mode has been laid out to deeply reform China's income distribution system and constantly increase the income of residents. Since the 18th CPC National Congress, the Chinese government has insisted on sharing development, made every effort to increase the income of residents, and strived to well achieve, maintain well and well develop the fundamental interests of all the people. In his speech at the First Session of the 12th National People's Congress on March 17, 2013, Xi Jinping said: "The people of our great country and the great times enjoy the opportunity to live together and enjoy the opportunity of a shared dream to come true and enjoy the opportunity to grow and make progress together with our motherland and the times."[8]

The Chinese government has firmly held the concept of shared development with economic construction as its center along the path of prosperity for all and has been committed to building a well-off society in an all-round way, and greatly improved the material and cultural living standards of all the people. Xi Jinping pointed out: "Sharing is the essential requirement of socialism with Chinese characteristics. We should follow the principle of the development for the people, the development by the people, the development fruits shared by the people, and make more effective institutional measures so that all the people can obtain more sense of fulfillment in achieving and sharing the development. We should increase the momentum of development, enhance the people's unity and head steadily towards prosperity for all."[9] The Chinese government has deepened the reform of income distribution system and promoted the increase of residents' income under the guidance of shared development.

8 The Party Literature Research Office of the CPC Central Committee, *Selected Important Literature After the 18th CPC National Congress*. Vol. 1, Central Party Literature Press, 2014, p. 235.
9 The Party Literature Research Office of the CPC Central Committee, *Selected Important Literature After the 18th CPC National Congress*. Vol. 2, Central Party Literature Press, 2014, p. 793.

The 19th CPC National Congress pointed out: "We will continue to follow the principle of distribution according to one's work while improving our institutions and mechanisms for distribution based on factors of production, so as to make income distribution fairer and more orderly. We will encourage people to make their money through hard work and legal means. We will expand the size of the middle-income group, increase income for people on low incomes, adjust excessive incomes, and prohibit illicit income. We will work to see that individual incomes grow in step with economic development and pay rises in tandem with increases in labor productivity which is also laborers' productive forces. We will expand the channels for people to make work-based earnings and property income." In recent years, the Chinese government has further improved the income distribution system in which distribution according to work is dominant and a variety of distribution modes coexist and has rationally adjusted the income distribution by all means of increasing the residents' income. The Chinese government has led the Chinese people to deepen reform of the income distribution system, enhance the primary distribution system, improve the re-distribution and regulation mechanism, standardize the income distribution order, increase the residents' property income, achieve the development results shared by all the people, and make great strides on the way to ultimately achieving prosperity for all.

1. The reform of the income distribution system has been deepened

The reform of income distribution system is a long-term systematic project. Therefore, we should deepen the reform of income distribution system, proceed joint development, and promote the sharing of development fruits. Deepening the reform income distribution system has a practical significance for increasing the income of Chinese residents and achieving the sustainable development of China's economy. The reform of China's income distribution system has highlighted the relationship between fairness and efficiency. We have worked well to see that individual incomes grow in step with economic development and pay rises in tandem with increases in labor productivity. We have continuously increased the disposable income of urban and rural residents. In the concrete level of income distribution, the Chinese government has standardized the primary distribution, intensified efforts to regulate income redistribution, adjusted and optimized the pattern of national income distribution, and narrowed the income gap throughout the whole society.

Since the 18th CPC National Congress, the Chinese government has focused on protecting labor income and increasing the proportion of labor payment in the primary distribution. The state has strengthened the institutional construction in the reform of income distribution system, improved the wage determination and normal growth mechanism, reformed the minimum wage and wage payment guarantee system, perfected the system of collective bargaining on wages, reformed the institutions' salary and subsidy system, and perfected the subsidy growth mechanism in border and impoverished areas. It has established and improved the remuneration mechanism based on capital, knowledge, technology, management and other factors of the market decision-making, expanded the investment and leasing services, optimized the payback mechanism of listed companies, protected the legitimate rights and interests of investors, especially small and medium-sized investors, and increased the income of residents' property by multi-channel. Through the enforcement of tax regulation, the mechanism of the redistribution regulation has been advanced, and the reasonable sharing mechanism of public resource transfer proceeds established. We have improved the system of tax reduction and exemption for charitable donations and supported the active role of charity in alleviating poverty and hardship.

In addition, to deepen the reform of income distribution system, the Chinese government has also enhanced the mechanism and policy system of income distribution regulation and set up personal income and property information system. It has also protected lawful income, regulated excessive income, cleaned up or standardized recessive income, prohibited illicit income, increased the income for low-income earners, enlarged the proportion of middle-income group, and narrowed the income distribution gap between urban and rural areas, between regions and between industries so that gradually has formed the "olive type" income distribution pattern in the society.

2. The primary distribution mechanism has been perfected

The primary distribution results in the basic income of residents. Under the guidance of shared development, the improvement of the primary distribution mechanism is an important foundation for the increase of residents' income with regards to efficiency and fairness. Xi Jinping pointed out emphatically: "We should uphold and improve the basic socialist distribution system and work hard to ensure that personal income grows in step with the economy, and that wages increase in step with labor productivity. We will adjust the national income distribution stricture, bring about consistent increases in the incomes of urban and rural residents, and continue to shrink the income gap, through constant improvement of systems and mechanisms as well as specific measures."[10]

To improve the primary distribution system, the emphasis is on enhancing the factors of labor, capital, technology, and management by their contribution to the primary distribution mechanism. Thus, the Chinese government has implemented employment priorities and more proactive employment policies, expanded the scale of employment and entrepreneurship, created an equal employment environment, enhanced laborers' capacity of earning income, and achieved higher-quality employment. Also, it has deepened the reform of wage system, improved the enterprise, institution wage decision and growth mechanism. It has promoted the equal use of factors of production, fair participation in market competition and legal protection of all kinds of ownership economy, which has formed the mechanism of determining the factor price of production mainly by the market.

Since the 18th CPC National Congress, the Chinese government has improved the contribution of market evaluation factors and the distribution mechanism according to the contribution in the aspect of the primary distribution mechanism. It has promoted the scientific salary level-decision mechanism, the normal growth mechanism, the payment guarantee mechanism, strengthened the classified supervision for the salary distribution of state-owned enterprises, put the system of collective bargaining on wages into effect, enhanced the minimum wage growth mechanism, improved the high-skilled personnel payment system, increased the income of skilled workers. It has advanced the wage system which fit to the characteristics of institutions. The Chinese government has highlighted the incentive function of income distribution policy, expanded the access of knowledge, technology and management and other elements to participate in distribution and increased the property income of urban and rural residents through multi-channel.

---

10   Develop China's Contemporary Marxist Political Economy based on China's National Conditions and Development Experience, *People's Daily*, November 25, 2015, p. 1.

3. The redistribution adjustment mechanism has been improved

Effective redistribution adjustment mechanism plays a significant role in adjusting income distribution, narrowing the income gap between people living in urban and rural areas, regional and social members, and promoting income distribution equity. Xi Jinping pointed out: "We should hold tightly on the socialist basic economic system and income distribution system, adjust the income distribution pattern, improve the redistribution mechanism, using taxation, social security and transfer payments as the main methods to appropriately adjust the distribution between urban and rural areas, regions and different groups. We should maintain social fairness and justice, solve the problem of income disparity, and ensure that the people benefit more from the achievements of reform."[11]

Since the 18th CPC National Congress, to advance the redistribution adjustment mechanism, the Chinese government has carried out policies which are advantageous to narrowing the income gap, obviously increasing the income of the low-income workers and enlarging the proportion of the middle-income earners. Improving the mechanism of redistribution adjustment aims at speeding up and advancing the mechanism, by using the major measures of tax, social security and transfer payments.

Therefore, the state has improved the public finance system, worked hard to perfect the transfer payment system, adjusted the structure of fiscal expenditure, and vigorously promoted the equalization of basic public services. As Xi Jinping emphatically pointed out: "We, all party members have to bear such an idea in mind: 'As long as there is a family and even a person who has not tackled the basic living problems, we will not feel ease. If the expectation of the people for a happy life has not become a reality, we will spare no efforts to lead the people together to achieve that goal."[12]

In terms of the tax system, the Chinese government has increased the tax regulation level, reformed the personal income tax policy, improved the property taxation system, promoted the structural tax reduction, eased the tax burdens of the middle-and low-income earners and small enterprises, and formulated

11   Comrade Xi Jinping's Remarks at the Symposium on Learning and Implementing the Spirit of the Fifth Plenary Session of the 18th CPC Central Committee for Leading Cadres at Provincial and Ministerial Levels, *People's Daily*, May 10, 2016, p. 1.

12   Xi Jinping, Extending the Blessings of the Chinese New Year on the Eve of the Spring Festival When Visiting and Doing Research in Inner Mongolia to All People, *People's Daily*, January 30, 2014, p. 1.

the tax system favorable for the structure optimization and social justice. The personal income tax system with the combination of integration and classification has been established, the tax burdens of middle and low-income earners have been reduced, and the excessive income been effectively regulated. At the same time, the Chinese government has taken some measures to levy the tax for high-end consumer goods and high consumption behavior.

In terms of social security, the Chinese government has enhanced tax policies with contribution to society and poverty relief. We have improved dynamic mechanism of securing basic needs of people with difficulties, and fully established the social security system covering urban and rural residents. The government has worked constantly to improve the social security, social assistance and social welfare systems based on the measures of total coverage, satisfying basic needs, multi-level and sustainability, with focus on enforcement on fairness, adapting to liquidity and ensuring sustainability to steadily improve the level of security and implement the integrated national social security card system.

In terms of transfer payments, the Chinese government has stepped up its efforts to effect transfer payments to the poverty-stricken groups in rural and urban areas, allocated more resources on the protection and improvement of the basic living needs of the poor rural and urban residents. The state has gradually increased proportion of state-owned capital gains in public finance, increased the public welfare expenditures, and the benefits from the transfer of the public resources were used to safeguard people's wellbeing.

4. The order of income distribution has been standardized

Since the 18th CPC National Congress, the Chinese government "adhered to focusing on efficiency and maintaining fairness. Both primary distribution and redistribution should take into account efficiency and fairness. Primary distribution should focus on efficiency, create a competitive environment with fair opportunities, and maintain the main position of labor income; redistribution should pay more attention to fairness, improve the efficiency of public resource allocation, and narrow the income gap."[13] On this basis, the Chinese government has strengthened the legal system in the field of income distribution and established a fair and reasonable income distribution order.

---

13 The Party Literature Research Office of the CPC Central Committee, *Selected Important Literature After the 18th CPC National Congress*. Vol. 1, Central Party Literature Press, 2014, p. 140.

The state has vigorously overhauled and standardized income distribution system, improved the current systems, perfected the laws and regulations, enforced the supervision on laws and regulations, strengthened the anti-corruption efforts, promoted information disclosure, implemented social supervision, emphasized the basic work, enhanced the technical security, protected lawful income, increased income for people with low-incomes, adjusted excessive incomes, regulated the hidden income and prohibited illicit incomes. Thus, it has effectively stopped obtaining income via the power, administrative monopoly and other non-market factors and standardized the level of income outside salary and non-monetary benefits. In recent years, the Chinese government has fully implemented non-cash settlement system, established and enhanced the natural person's income and property information system and advanced the income statistic investigation and monitoring system.

5. Residents' property income has been increased

Increasing the income of urban and rural residents is an important key to improve people's wellbeing in society building in China, which embodies the essential requirement of "putting the people at the center". Since the 18th CPC National Congress, the Chinese government has issued a series of regulations to increase the income of urban and rural residents, which provided policy guarantee for increasing the income of urban and rural residents. In October 2016, the State Council has enacted *Suggestions on The implementation of the State Council on Stimulating the Vitality of Key Groups to Promote the Income of Urban and Rural Residents*, focusing on stimulating the income-generating vitality of seven key groups including skillful talents, professional new farmers, scientific research personnel, small & micro-entrepreneurs, business managers and executives, community officials, the difficult groups with labor capacity, and implemented targeted programs to guide urban and rural residents to achieve overall income increase. In November 2016, *Suggestions of CPC Central Committee and State Council on Improving the Property Rights Protection System and Protecting Property Rights by Law*, was officially issued, which is the first decree that China has issued on the protection of property rights in the name of the central government, and which says, for the first time, the property rights of non-public economy and the property rights of public economy are equally inviolable. The decree has stipulated that all relevant systems should be improved to raise the property income of urban and rural residents, including the legal arrangements for the follow-up period of due land use rights of residential construction sites, deepening the reform of state-owned enterprises, financial reform, rural land reform and so on. To increase the income of urban and rural residents, the Chinese government has further deepened the reform, strengthened the legislation, enforced the system, and effectively protected the residents' lawful property and property income.

Increasing the residents' property income is ultimately to promote the common development of all people and share the fruits of development. In accordance with the strategic measures of CPC Central Committee to increase the residents' income by all means, the Chinese government has deepened the reform of income distribution system, optimized the income distribution structure, mobilized passions of all sides, promoted the transformation of economic development pattern, sustained social fairness, justice and harmonious stability, generally achieved the development benefits shared by the people, and laid a solid foundation for building a well-off society in an all-round way. In the process of promoting residents' property income, the Chinese government has constantly advocated working hard to get rich, supported the innovation and pioneering work, protected the lawful operation, and promoted the increase of social wealth and comprehensive national strength, while achieving the increase of people's income and the affluence of the people.

The Chinese government has made resolute efforts to boost the property income of residents. It has moved forward the reform of interest rate marketization, expanded the floating range of deposit and loan interest rate, protected the depositor's rights, and regularized bank charging behavior.

Moreover, the multi-level capital market has been developed, the dividend system of listed companies has been implemented, and the supervision measures have been strengthened to protect the legitimate rights and interests of investors, especially small and medium investors. The state has also pushed forward qualified enterprises to implement employee stock ownership plan, broadened income-raising channels such as the residents' rents, stocking interests, dividends and so on, enriched the funds products like bond funds, money funds and others. The Chinese government has steadily incorporated the social insurance fund into the capital market and classified the investment income into the integrated fund and individual account to preserve or increase its value.

III. Perfecting the social security system covering urban and rural areas

Social security system is a basic system to regulate social distribution and guarantee people's life. Since the 18th CPC National Congress, the Chinese government has attached immense importance to the construction of social security system. The *Decision of the CPC Central Committee on Some Major Issues Concerning Comprehensively Deepening the Reform* pointed out: "A more equitable and sustainable social security system should be established". Xi Jinping pointed out: "The work of securing and improving the wellbeing of the people will never end. Instead, there are always new starting points and we should achieve a positive cycle of economic development and improvement of people's wellbeing".[14] The 19th CPC National Congress pointed out: "We will act on the policy requirements to help those most in need, to build a tightly woven safety net, and to build the necessary institutions, as we work to develop a sustainable multi-tiered social security system that covers the entire population in both urban and rural areas, with clearly defined rights and responsibilities, and support that hits the right level." Guided by this spirit of the CPC Central Committee, the Chinese government has persisted in the basic principles of full coverage, urban and rural coordination, clear responsibility, moderate and sustainable social security, steadily enhanced the overall level and standard of China's social security, and basically established a more equitable and sustainable social security system covering urban and rural residents.

In recent years, the Chinese government has made great achievements in social security work. In the past five years, China's social security system has been gradually improved, with its coverage continuously expanded, its security level steadily enhanced, and its management and service optimized and standardized. China has built the world's largest social security system, and Chinese people are enjoying a stronger sense of fulfillment, of happiness and of security. In recent years, China has carried out the largest and widest nationwide insurance registration in the history of human social security, found out the basic number of insured people, established a nationwide insurance database covering 1.39 billion people, succeeded in obtaining

---

14   Strive to Promote Economic Development in Stability and Safeguard Improvement of People's Wellbeing, *People's Daily*, May 16, 2013.

the targeted key groups 'participation in insurance, and kept expanding the scope of various social insurance. By the end of October 2020, the coverage of basic endowment insurance, unemployment insurance and work-related injury insurance in China had reached 992 million, 214 million and 264 million respectively, all of which had completed the goal set in the 13th Five-Year plan ahead of schedule. A total of 59.49 million poverty-stricken people who had been filed and had registration cards participated in the basic endowment insurance, with the participation rate of more than 99.99%, basically realizing the full coverage. At present, the total number of people participating in the basic endowment insurance in China accounts for one third of the worldwide endowment coverage, forming the world's largest endowment insurance system. By the end of November 2020, the number of social security card holders in China had reached 1.332 billion, covering 95% of its population and all cities, and the 13th Five-Year Plan target was overfulfilled ahead of schedule. At the same time, the number of electronic security cards nationwide reached 314 million, and users can receive related through 419 APPs and online programs. China's basic medical insurance has more than 1.332 billion participants, and the coverage rate is stable at over 95%, making it the largest basic medical insurance network in the world. China's achievements in the development of social security system covering the urban and rural areas have been fully affirmed and highly appreciated by the international community, and the International Social Security Association has given its prestigious Award for Outstanding Achievements in Social Security to the Chinese government. The award offers worldwide recognition of a country's political commitment and long-term results in the field of social security. Hans-Horst Konkolewsky, the Secretary-General of the International Social Security Association, said, "if China is not counted, the world's social security coverage is only 50%, and if counted, the world coverage is 61%. As a result, China's contribution to the world's social security is enormous, playing a model role for other countries."[15]

---

15 Bai Tianliang, The Chinese Government was Awarded the International Social Security Outstanding Achievement Award, *People's Daily*, November 19, 2016, p. 6.

1. The social insurance system has been perfected

Since the 18th CPC National Congress, adhering to "putting people at the center", the Chinese government has enabled all people to enjoy the benefits of development and improved the social insurance system. In aspect of enforcing and advancing the construction of social insurance system, the Chinese government has implemented the plan of overall participation in social insurance and basically achieved the full coverage of the legal personnel. Moreover, it has worked well to keep actuarial balance, improve the fund-raising mechanism, clear the responsibilities among government, enterprises and individuals and made the appropriate reduction on social insurance fee rates. Xi Jinping is particularly concerned about China's parent-supporting problem. On New Year's Eve in 2014 in Beijing, Xi Jinping visited the frontline workers and elderly people and emphasized: "We should upgrade the system and improve our work and push forward the diversified development of the pension undertakings so that all senior citizens are respected, cared for and live happily in their later years." In order to perfect the social insurance system, the Chinese government has improved the overall plan of pension schemes, enhanced the ability of the social insurance management service, and strengthened the supervision and management on the social security fund.

First, the Chinese government has issued the general plan for implementing and promoting basic pension schemes. The approach to implementing enterprise annuity is introduced, and the reform of old-age insurance system for government agencies and institutions is further advanced. To press ahead with the reform of the pension insurance system for government agencies and institutions, to establish a more equitable basic old-age insurance system, the *Decision on the Reform of the Pension Insurance System for Staff in Government Organs and Public Institutions* was issued by the State Council in January 2015. This proposal put forward a feasible solution to the problem of the dual system of pension insurance, which is a breakthrough in the construction of China's old-age insurance system.

The development of the urban and rural pension system has been comprehensively improved, and the system and regulation equity has been enforced. In recent years, the Chinese government has made constant efforts to improve the basic old-age insurance system covering urban and town employees based on integration of social pool planning with personal account, established a multi-level old-age insurance system, including occupational annuity, enterprise annuity, commercial insurance and so on, extended the coverage of social insurance, and basically realized the whole national plan of basic pension for employees. Moreover, the Chinese government has improved the personal account system of the employees' pension insurance, perfected the incentive and restraint mechanism of the insured payment, built the reasonable adjustment mechanism of the basic pension and at proper time introduced tax deferred pension insurance. It is better to make the best of unemployment and work-related injury insurance, enforce the flexibility of the rate pricing, optimize and adjust the application scope. A more convenient mechanism of social insurance transfer and succession has been established. The government has transferred some state-owned capital to enrich the social security fund, broadened the social insurance fund investment channels, reinforced the risk management and increased the return on investment. The proportion of social insurance by the flexible employment workers and migrant workers has been greatly enhanced, the construction of the public service facility and the information platform have been improved. The social security card project has been implemented to greatly increase the coverage numbers of social security card cardholders.

Second, the social insurance management service has been improved. in February 2014, the Chinese government passed the decree Comments of the State Council on the Establishment of An Integrated Basic Pension Insurance System for Urban and Rural Residents, emphasizing the solution to the problem of the urban-rural division on old-age insurance by strengthening fairness, adapting to liquidity and maintaining sustainability, and speeding up the overall construction of a fair and unified old-age insurance system covering urban and rural residents. In the light of specific measures, the national remote medical network settlement system has been established and the goal of the direct settlement of remote medical costs in accordance with the referral requirements has basically been achieved. The reform of the registration system of "Five Certificates in Unity" has been pushed forward. The standardization system of social security service has been improved. The management measures and service methods have been introduced. The pace of electronic social security construction has been accelerated. The Standardization, informatization and professionalization level has been enhanced. The Chinese government has comprehensively implemented the national insurance coverage plan, ensured the pension payment on time and in full, and basically completed the national database of full insurance coverage.

The commercial pension insurance is booming, and social pension security system has been improved. The Chinese government has pushed the commercial insurance institutions to offer personalized and differentiated pension security for individuals and families, to provide enterprises and occupational annuity products and services, and to promote the diversified development of the elderly care service industry. It has also developed some commercial pension insurance such as the aged accident injury, long-term care, housing reverse mortgage insurances and others, has set up pension service security system including long-term care service, treatment combined with attendance, medical care with health maintenance and so on. It has ensured the secure and reliable operation of the commercial pension insurance fund and attained the value-preserving and reasonable return. Furthermore, the commercial pension insurance funds have been encouraged to be invested in new, equity, trusteeship, and other ways to set up nursing homes for the elderly. Meanwhile, the government has implemented the relevant fiscal and taxation policies of the state-supported insurance and the elderly care service industry, accelerated the development of pilot program about the deferred personal tax on commercial pension insurance, supported the commercial pension insurance organization to orderly participate in the basic pension insurance fund investment management, provided the green channel and the preferential support for the commercial pension insurance fund in investment in the national important project and the people's wellbeing project and so on. The goal of "the elderly should be cared for" has been achieved via the development of commercial pension insurance measures and great progress in the social security system.

Third, the supervision and management of social security fund were streamlined. The Chinese government has strengthened the construction of the social supervision teams and improved the working mechanism on the convergence of social supervision and administrative supervision. The state has promoted the supervision standard, urged social security and insurance institutions to enhance service quality, safeguarded the legitimate rights and interests of consumers, and effectively prevented and controlled all kinds of risks. The Chinese government has also improved the investment operation mechanism of basic pension insurance fund, simultaneously enhanced the fund-supporting capacity with multiple measures, reinforced the collaboration with public security institutions, improved the investigation and supervision in respect to social security fraud cases and timely dealing with the illegal criminal cases according to law. The monitoring and supervision measures in respect to administering social security fund were strengthened.

First, the laws and regulations in respect to social security fund supervision were upgraded. The establishment of a levy system linked to the tax and social security fund has provided a reliable source for the social security fund levying and guaranteed the adequacy of the social security fund. Secondly, the IT application of the social security fund system was improved.

With the rapid increase of payments from the social security fund, the government has raised the IT application level for the supervision of social security fund, achieved the digital IT administration of the social security fund data, updated the fund data in real time thus achieved a dynamic administration, reduced the risk for the social security fund and the maintenance of the relevant data of the social security fund has been improved to ensure the security and accuracy of the data. Then, the transparency of regulatory information has been enhanced. The relevant regulations about supervising the information disclosure of social security funds have been improved. The information disclosure system has been enforced and the procedures of information disclosure has been standardized. At the same time, employees' sense of responsibility has been improved to ensure the veracity and authoritativeness of the social security funds information disclosed. Finally, the market supervision on the social security funds has been intensified. Some professionals have been introduced to establish a third-party supervision and management team to improve the supervision level through the surveillance on the operation of social security funds in all aspects by the third party.

2. The social assistance system has been improved

Social assistance is a supportive measure and basic system design of the social security system, and the sound social assistance system plays a key role in maintaining the bottom line of social fairness, eliminating the survival crisis of those groups in difficulty thus achieving the social harmony and social stability.

On June 7, 2017, officials from Chiping County, Shandong province launched "The Elderly Care with Respects and Duties" fund ceremony in Changzhuang and Han Xi Village, Hantun Town so that the elderly here could be relieved from poverty and cared for. The campaign injected new energy for the current targeted poverty reduction.

Since the 18th CPC National Congress, the Chinese government has adhered to innovative thinking and improved the social assistance system. It has promoted the construction of urban and rural social assistance system, upgraded the minimum living security system, strengthened the policy convergence, advanced the system integration and ensured the basic living of people with difficulties. In accordance with the general idea of "meeting basic needs, prioritizing key areas, improving institutions, and guiding public expectations", the social assistance system has been enhanced and the basic wellbeing security level has been increased. When he attended the deliberations of the delegation from Hunan Province at the Fourth Session of the 12th National People's Congress, Xi Jinping emphasized: "We must grasp structural reforms with one hand and making up for the shortcomings of people's wellbeing with the other, properly adjust the financial expenditure structure, effectively safeguard the basic wellbeing of the masses, guarantee the basic public services, resolutely guard the bottom-line of people's wellbeing, and resolutely win the battle against poverty. We should promote the coordinated construction of a social assistance system covering urban and rural areas so that the people in need will have access to help and timely assistance." In recent years, the Chinese government has strengthened the social assistance system and other social security systems, linked the special assistance with and the low-income assistance, enriched the relief service content, reasonably increased the relief standard and established the comprehensive relief work pattern. To improve the social assistance system, the Chinese government has focused on the following five aspects:

First, overall planning and improving the social assistance system. The Chinese government has strengthened the integrated social assistance system and achieved the transition from single aid to comprehensive relief. It has also intensified the integration with the related social security system and focused on the integration of the rural minimum subsistence and the policy of poverty alleviation and on the integration of the medical assistance to severe diseases and the critical illness insurance. It has pushed forward the coordinated development of urban and rural areas with the realization of urban and rural co-ordination about medical assistance, temporary relief, low-income relief and special hardship support.

Second, the targeted identifying and sound social assistance mechanism. The Chinese government has enforced the social assistance family economic status check mechanism, worked well in the precise identification of the target, and strived to achieve the timely assistance and relief. The state has intensified the working mechanism of "emergency aid", built the all-round "emergency aid" pilot, strengthened the community-based homeless begging relief and service facility construction, enabled the dispersed social assistance resources to work together and enhanced the relief benefits. It has strengthened the mechanism of "accepted by one department and handled by the cooperated ones", truly has achieved that people with difficulties can find somewhere to seek help and get prompt aid.

Third, prioritizing key areas and enhancing the function of social assistance to see basic needs are met. Key areas have been prioritized and precise measures have been taken to provide assistance. The focus is on providing more personalized and differentiated services for the elderly, the disabled, minors, the seriously ill and other individuals with special difficulties among the recipients of assistance, bringing into play the role of social assistance to see basic needs are met. Precisely and efficient, scientific screening of the causes of poverty, actual needs and degree of difficulty of the needy groups, etc., and timely and appropriate adjustment of the level of assistance. The key institutions has been improved so that different categories of hardship groups with different needs are covered by the system.

Fourth, sharing the information and strengthening the comprehensive social relief. The government has promoted sharing the information about social assistance and relief management among departments, avoiding the repetition or missing of assistance and relief. It has made more progress in comprehensive social assistance, assistance surroundings and mechanism, appealed more social forces, marketing subjects, as well as voluntary individuals to participate in social assistance and given full play to the unique advantages of social forces and marketing subjects, as well as volunteers to form an effective supplement to government assistance and strengthen the comprehensive assistance from the government and social forces, main market players as well as the volunteers and so on.

Fifth, enforcing the supervision and promoting fairness and equity of social assistance. Strengthening supervision is an effective measure to promote the fairness and justice of social relief work. Focusing on self-monitoring and social supervision, social relief work has developed with open policy, transparent process and fair results. The government has put emphasis on the rule of law and strict disciplines, seriously dealt with the violation of the law and discipline of social assistance to ensure the fairness and justice of social assistance.

3. The social welfare system has been strengthened

Social welfare system is one of the important contents of social security system. Improving social welfare system will help to build the social security system covering the urban and rural residents, help to guarantee the harmonious and stable development of the whole society, and help to fulfill the goal of a moderately prosperous society in an all-round way. China's social welfare system mainly aims at providing material supplies, social services or monetary subsidies for the disadvantaged groups to enhance their self-reliance capacity and improve their living standards.

Since the 18th CPC National Congress, the Chinese government has upgraded the social welfare system, which focuses on the assistance to the old, disabled, the young, and the special people with difficulties. The specific measures taken by the Chinese government to strengthen the social welfare system include are the following three:

Firstly, moving forward the household-based welfare service in all respects. The family support policy has been formulated, and the function of family support for the old and young is strengthened and the welfare of children with difficulties has been improved. In addition, we have enhanced child adoption system and pushed forward overall promotion of family-care services for the senior citizens. Relying on the purchase of services by community, government and social forces, we have provided living care, domestic service, rehabilitation care and spiritual comforting care, and many other services for the elderly at home. We have adopted a variety of rearing modes, such as rearing by relatives, citizen adoption, family foster care, social support, and so on, to promote the healthy growth of orphans and disabled children in the environment full of affection. Special projects have been carried out including free surgeries for the disabled orphans in the country, free operations for children with cleft lip and palate in poor families, and the medical treatment for children with cerebral palsy in social welfare institutions to restore nearly 100,000 children to health and to family and society.

Secondly, the infrastructure of social welfare institutions has been improved. The government has accelerated the reform of public welfare institutions, strengthened the construction of welfare facilities, optimized the layout of welfare facilities and promoted the sharing of welfare resources. In recent years, the number of social welfare institutions run by the Chinese government has been increasing continuously, with their functions more improved and infrastructure conditions getting better. The private social welfare institutions have developed rapidly with the growth number increasing fast and the good conditions in all aspects, which have played a key role in the provision of social welfare.

Thirdly, the community-based welfare service has been greatly developed. Xi Jinping pointed out: "Yes, the community is small, but it affects millions of households. The community party organizations and members should make every possible effort to facilitate people's living, help people express their appeals more smoothly and openly, and convey the care from party and the government to the innumerable households."[16] Therefore, the Chinese government has established and improved the elderly-care service facilities

---

16   Xi Jinping, Extending the Blessings of the Chinese New Year on the Eve of the Spring Festival When Visiting and Doing Research in Inner Mongolia to All People, *People's Daily*, January 30, 2014, p. 1.

in the streets and communities, provided various basic services such as living and family services, emergency assistance, day care, rehabilitation health-care, recreational service and so on, which are popular among the elderly. The care and resettlement affairs, non-profit basic funeral services, the funeral homes, non-profit ash-placing and interment facilities and the construction of public cemeteries was further improved. Furthermore, the development of community welfare services for the disabled has been promoted, the rehabilitation of the disabled in communities has been improved and the capacity of the disabled people to participate in society has been increased. Some children's welfare institutions also take their own advantages to offer services to their communities and to tackle problems from families with disabled children.

4. The development of social charity undertakings has been advanced

Since the 18th CPC National Congress, China's charity associations has boomed with the participation of various strata and groups interested in charity projects represented by charity associations developing rapidly. The social charity awareness has been enhanced, and all kinds of charity campaigns have been actively launched, playing a positive role in the fields of public undertakings such as the disaster relief, poverty relief, medical assistance, aids for the old and disabled and the like.

The Chinese government has further pushed the development of charitable and professional social work, mobilized social forces in a large scale to carry out social relief, social assistance and voluntary services, and improved the regular social donation mechanism. *The Recommendations of the CPC Central Committee on the Formulation of the 13th Five-Year Plan for National Economic and Social Development* emphasized: "We should sustain the development of social philanthropy and broadly mobilize social forces to carry out social relief, social assistance and voluntary service activities. We should improve and issue the tax policies to benefit back society and to favor people with difficulties.

The development of social charity has been promoted. We have vigorously developed charity organizations, simplified the approval procedure of charity organizations, and encouraged qualified enterprises, individuals and social organizations to involve in public welfare undertakings such as hospitals, schools and the elderly-care services. We have also strengthened the charity organization supervision and management, implemented and improved the charity donation tax preferential policies, which permits the carry-over after the annual deduction over 12% of the enterprises' charity donation expenditure surpassing the annual total profit.

We have pushed forward the legislative work to promote the development of charity undertakings. To develop social charity, carry forward charity culture, standardize charity activities, protect the legitimate rights and interests of charity organizations, donors, volunteers and beneficiaries, promote social progress and share the fruits of development, *The Charity Law of the People's Republic of China* was passed at the Fourth Session of the 12th National People's Congress on March 16, 2016. The enactment of *The Charity Law of People's Republic of China* indicates the development of China's charity has entered a stage ruled by laws.

In recent years, the development of philanthropy in China has made remarkable achievements. "More than 10 years, the philanthropy in China has rapidly grew with annual charity donations from less than tens of billions of dollars 10 years ago to the current hundreds of billions of dollars, with more than 600,000 social organizations registered in the Civil Affairs Department, most of which are in the field of charity, with millions of the charity projects in total, and with hundreds of millions of beneficiaries each year."[17] Among these notable achievements, the community-based "Children's Home" service model in Mudanjiang, Heilongjiang Province, and the "integrated promotion model of children's life and growth" in Wuxi, Jiangsu Province, are especially worth mentioning in terms of children's welfare.

In 2012, the Children's Welfare House in Mudanjiang City was designated as a pilot agency by the Ministry of Civil Affairs in collaboration with United Nations Children's Fund on the "community services for children in distress" project. After three-year practice, the house has explored in the community "Children's Home" service model based on "the unity of home, family and society", which was highly praised by the Ministry of Civil Affairs and the United Nations Children's Fund and won good reputation from families of children with difficulties and other fields in society.

To work well with activities in the "Children's Home", three service teams were introduced to children's home. One is the professional team of institutions composed of professionals in welfare institutions who have the qualifications of rehabilitation, education, psychology and childcare; Another team is the social worker team made of recruited professional social workers with

---

17 Yu Jianwei, Boost Charity Development According to the Rule of Law, *People's Daily*, March 22, 2016, p. 11.

social working experience and the staff in institutions with the social working qualifications. The third is a volunteer team, that is, a "children's home" volunteer service team which has been established on the cooperation with the League and City committee, colleges and institutions, hospitals with the recruited professionals in the fields of education, medical care and laws. The establishment of three service teams not only meets service needs for the community "Children's Home" but also enhances the service capacity and professional level of the staff in the welfare house.

While the pilot project is being carried out, the institute has set up a network of child welfare organizations in Mudanjiang city to promote the construction of "children's home" in the city. By the end of 2014, in Mudanjiang City and its 5 counties (towns), the urban community "children's home" construction rate had reached 100%, with more than 2000 statistically-registered children in plight. Over the past three years, the project has provided services for more than 200 children and parents, organized the community, group activities for 35 times with the case services for 1000 individuals. In a word, the children and their families with difficulties, institutions, communities, volunteers all have benefited from the project.[18]

Similarly, the "integrated promotion model of children's life and growth" implemented by Wuxi Children's Welfare Institution in Jiangsu Province has also been highly praised by the society.

Located at Xigang Road, Xishan District, Wuxi City, Wuxi Children's Welfare Institute was built in 2010 with the total investment of nearly RMB 80 million and the covered area of 13591 square meters. It has the beautiful courtyard environment, multi-functional facilities, and children-friendly internal design.

In recent years, Wuxi Children's Welfare House has actively explored and established the people-oriented philosophy and children's interest priority principle, has integrated all work based on the unity of medical care, nursing, rehabilitation, education and social workers, has paid more attention to children's five needs for life growth and has emphasized more on an individual's harmonious development. Here, every child's life rights can be guaranteed, every child's life needs can be satisfied, and every child's life development can be concerned for.[19]

---

18 Zhang Lirong, The Seeds of 'Children's Home' Blossom and Bear Fruits in the Community, *Social Welfare*, 2015(7).
19 Children's Welfare Institution in Wuxi: The Integration for Promoting Children's Life, *Social Welfare*, 2015(7).

Chapter Four

Building A Social Governance System with Chinese Characteristics

Social governance is an important aspect of society building. Social governance is a process in which various social subjects participate in social affairs. In this process, various governance subjects, such as government, enterprises and institutions, social organizations, communities, villages and individuals, regulate and guide social organizations, social affairs and social life based on laws and regulations through equal cooperation, consultation, communication and dialogue. The ultimate purpose of social governance is to achieve the maximization of the public interest. Social governance pays particular attention to scientificity and systematicity, focusing on the flexibility of working methods, and is rigid and flexible, taking into account the prevention of social conflicts and the resolution of social conflicts, and ultimately achieving a stable, healthy and sustainable development of the society. To strengthen social governance, we have to improve the government's governance capacity and level, increase the service functions of communities, give full play to the role of social organizations, increase self-regulation function of the society, and perfect the public participation mechanism and improve the mechanisms to protect rights and interests and resolve conflicts. The construction of the social governance system with Chinese characteristics should focus on strengthening the construction of social governance system, building the basic public services system, constructing a modern social organization system, continually strengthening and innovating the social governance mechanism so as to gradually achieve good governance in the governance of the society.

I.　Strengthening the construction of a social governance system

About strengthening the construction of social governance mechanism, Xi Jinping pointed out in his report to the 19th CPC National Congress: "We will step up institution building in social governance and improve the law-based social governance model under which Party committees exercise leadership, government assumes responsibility, non-governmental actors provide assistance [social collaboration], and the public get involved. We will strengthen public participation and rule of law [guarantees] in social governance, and make such governance smarter and more specialized." In this statement, the essence of the "leadership exercised by Party Committees" is ensuring the realization of the people's interests and will and organizing and supporting the people to make their own decisions as masters. In the adherence to the leadership exercised by Party Committees and innovating social governance, the key lies in to continuously advance the transformation in the way the Party exercises leadership and governance from the Party-rule-led type to the rule of law-led type and from the power-led type to authority-led type. Government taking responsibility means improving the function and working of the government so as to promote the government's transformation into a honest and highly efficient service-oriented government whose functions are scientific and whose structure is optimized and which people are satisfied with. Such government plays the leading role in social governance, responsible for the people and seeking profits for the people. "Non-governmental actors provide assistance [social collaboration], and the public get involved [public participation]" is a great highlight of the social governance during the new historical period, and is also an area that needs more focus and investment in strengthening the construction of social governance system. The concept of "rule of law guarantees" is focused on maintaining the social fairness and justice and guaranteeing that the masses enjoy extensive rights and freedoms in accordance with the law. Strengthening the construction of the social governance system should be carried out in an orderly manner under the premise of rule of law guarantees.

1. The way the Communist Party of China exercises leadership has been improved

In order to improve the way the Communist Party of China exercises leadership, we should first advance the transformation in the way the Party exercises leadership from the Party-rule-led type to the rule of law-led type. It is pointed out in the report of the 18th CPC National Congress that the Party leads people to enact the Constitution and the laws and the Party must act under the constraints of Constitution and laws. No organization or individual is privileged to perform beyond the Constitution and laws. Under no circumstance can the law be replaced by any individual's speech, suppressed by power or bent for personal gains. In the transformation in the way the Party exercises leadership from the Party-rule-led type to the rule of law-led type, the emphasis is on changing the former practice of Party governing gradually into law-based governance. Law-based governance refers to defining in the form of law the status and functions of the ruling party and participating parties in the whole country and social politic systems, regulating the responsibilities and functions of the ruling party and state legislature, judicial and administrative authorities and their mutual relationship and finally making the national public power take the responsibility and act in line with the law. The Party's leadership is the basic guarantee of people being the master of the country and law-based governance. That people are the master of the country is the essence and core of socialist democratic politics. Law-based governance is the basic strategy of the Party leading the people to govern the country. We should give a full play of the Party's directing the overall situation and coordinating the efforts from all quarters, improve and perfect the way the Party exercises leadership and governance so as to continually raise the Party's level of exercising political power in accordance with science, democracy and law."[1] By transforming the way it exercises leadership, the Communist Party of China has gradually achieved the law-based exercise of leadership and truly achieved the law-based rule of the country and administration.

To improve the way the CPC exercises leadership, the next step is to advance the transformation in the way the Party exercises leadership and

---

1 *A Series of Important Speeches by General Secretary Xi Jinping* (2016 ed.), compiled by the Publicity Department of the CPC Central Committee, People's Press, 2016, p. 164-165.

governance from the power-led type to authority-led type. The so-called power-led type refers to the past mechanism of controlling and managing the whole society by relying on a power-based form. The salient feature of this mechanism is that in controlling and managing the entire society the effect of power is quite outstanding and even exceeds the boundaries of power and can cause disharmony and instability in the society to some extent. Therefore, in the process of building a governance system with Chinese characteristics and enhancing the construction of social governance, the Communist Party of China gradually eliminates the way of such power-led type control and management of the society and advances the gradual transformation from the power-led type to the authority-led type. The authority-led type means the Party's governance of the entire society is established on the basis of effectively guaranteeing people's democratic rights, and truly accomplishing "putting the people at the center", representing the basic interests of the overwhelming majority of the people and practicing the principle of serving the people whole-heartedly. Meanwhile, in the process of governance of the entire society, civil servants engaged in social governance rely on their exemplary behavior to win the support of the broad masses of the people, enhance the Party's ability to politically unite, to politically appeal and its political authority, forming a stable and harmonious social governance and social operation mechanism. Therefore, the way the Communist Party of China exercises leadership has been improved and the construction of China's social governance system has been strengthened.

2. A service-oriented government for the satisfaction of the people has been constructed

The Constitution of the People's Republic of China has specified regulations about power belonging and government responsibility such as "All power in the People's Republic of China belongs to the people", "The people administer state affairs and manage economic and cultural undertakings and social affairs through various channels and in various ways in accordance with the provisions of law", "The National People's Congress and the local People's Congresses at various levels are constituted through democratic elections, responsible for the people and subject to their supervision", "All administrative, judicial and prosecuting organs of the State are created by the people's congresses for which they are responsible and by which they are supervised". In line with the above provisions of *The Constitution of the People's Republic of China*, people are the master of the country and government officials, and staff serve people. Thus, the Chinese government is one that maintains and realizes people's interests as well as serves people. Building a people-satisfied government is the basic requirement of the Chinese government exercising its administration and carrying out its policies. In March 2013, in the *Circular of the General Office of State Council on Task Division in Implementation of the "Proposals of the State Council for Institutional Reforms and Functional Transformation"* it was pointed out that "it is planned to take three to five years to fulfill the tasks mentioned in the *Proposals* and it is planned to speed up the construction of an honest and highly efficient service-oriented government whose functions are scientific and structures are optimized and that people are satisfied with". Adhering to the concept of "government responsibility" in strengthening the social governance system as pointed out by the 19th CPC National Congress, the Chinese government, guided by this concept, constructed a service-oriented government for the satisfaction of the people mainly in the following three aspects:

First of all, in order to build a service-oriented government for the satisfaction of the people, Chinese government officials and employees have changed their ideas and taken practical actions. Since the 18th National People's Congress, Chinese government officials and employees have changed not only their ideas but also their roles. Moreover, they have gradually set up a new concept that government plays a role of social administrator and public product provider. And they have built and perfected the public approval institution, and public financial system. In perfecting the public institution of examination and approval, the government lays great emphasis on the institution construction for examination and approval and gives extra help and support to the plans involving public service and products, strengthening the examination and approval of such kind of programs. The key point in perfecting the public financial institution lies in that the public finance is shifted to provide the society with more public products and service, and continually promoting and realizing the equal distribution of public products and services. The Chinese government performs its public service function, and truly plays its role of social governor and provider of public products. The Chinese government has strengthened the construction of government information publicity, expanded people's supervision of the government through the network. The Chinese government also actively accelerates electronic government construction, promotes and perfects government online working. Promoting the progress of the government's online and paperless working has helped to build a service-oriented government which satisfies the people's needs.

Secondly, in order to build a service-oriented government to better serve the people, the government has enhanced the ability of providing public goods and services, and raised the social governance level. In the historical course of building a moderately prosperous society in all aspects, the Chinese government has actively strengthened the capability of supplying public goods, began to provide more and more public goods and enhanced the social governance. The most important aspect of public goods is that they serve the public order and social security, which can be provided only by the state rather than any social organizations or individual. When providing these public goods, the government has formulated its public policy, maintains social order, social security, and strengthens social governance. Besides, the Chinese government has also increased the ability of supplying public goods including social security, science, culture and education, health care, social welfare thus satisfied the people's growing material and cultural life needs, all of which have elevated social governance to a new level.

Thirdly, in order to build a service-oriented government which satisfies the people's needs, the government has improved its public service ability and innovated social governance. Since the 18th CPC National Congress, the Chinese government has enhanced its public service ability of adjusting social interests, solving social problems and dealing with social conflicts and maintaining social stability. According to Marxism, social contradictions exist anywhere and anytime, and human society has been developing and progressing in contradictions. An important feature of building a moderately prosperous society in all aspects is the need to constantly advance in the process of resolving social conflicts. Properly adjusting different interests is a vital measure to resolve social contradictions. Thus, the Chinese government has been constantly improving the ability to provide public service and innovate social governance, maintaining social harmony and stability by solving social problems and dealing with social contradictions and gradually promoting the construction of a moderately prosperous society in all aspects. In this way, Chinese government has gradually and steadily transformed into a service-oriented government for the satisfaction of the people.

3. Social collaboration has been enhanced

Social collaboration refers to the clear work division among the People's Congress, the Chinese People's Political Consultative Conference (CPPCC), the Federation of Labor Unions, the Communist League, the Federation of Women, social organizations and self-government organizations at grassroots levels in order to achieve the construction of a virtuous mechanism of social governance which is interconnected and interactive so as to promote all parties involved in social governance to work together and develop a situation of co-governance and good governance. Through effective social coordination mechanism, the social parties concerned fully play their roles in social governance, provide services, regulate behaviors, reflect people's demands and strengthen the social governance by making the

On December 2, 2016, on the 5th National Traffic Safety Day, the Beijing Public Bureau, Traffic Management Bureau, Police Air Corps, the Beijing Red Cross 999 Emergency Center launched a coordinated drill of rescue and relief following the serious accidents on Jingkun expressway in Fangshan District.

parties concerned interact positively. Social collaboration is a vital theme of innovating the construction of social governance.

Giving full play to social collaboration. A pattern of multi-lateral participation and common governance under the leadership of the Party committees and the government has been formed, giving play to the collaborative, interactive and complementary role of multiple main intermediate bodies such as the market, social organizations, citizens and individuals in the construction of the social governance system. The participation of trade unions, the Communist Youth League, women's federations and other people's organizations and mass organizations in the construction of the social governance system has been strengthened and a favorable environment and conditions for them to play their role has been actively created. The cultivation and support to social organizations such as industry associations, chamber of commerce, science and technology organizations, public charity, rural and urban community service have been intensified. Duties related to the construction of social governance mechanism including conflict appeasement, dispute mediation, management of service for special groups and the precaution of juvenile delinquency which are suitable to be undertaken by social organizations are put on the list of government's payments for the service and assigned to the relevant social organizations to make them play their important role in the construction of social governance. Since the 18th CPC National Congress, social collaboration has become an important innovation and attraction in social governance system. The important roles of social collaboration are displayed in the following four aspects:

First, the People's Congresses of all levels exert their role of social governance supervision as authoritative organs related to social governance. The National People's Congress and local People's Congresses at all levels have passed a series of new laws and regulations concerning social governance at the national and local levels, which have enhanced the institutionalization and standardization of social governance. At the same time, the National People's Congress and local People's Congresses at all levels began to actively play their supervisory role in social governance, urging the local governments of all levels to strengthen social governance and safeguard the public security, thus have promoted synergy in the development of social governance.

Second, the People's Political Consultative Conferences at all levels play an important role of "social consultation" in the process of social governance. The National People's Political Consultative Conference and the local People's Political Consultative Conferences at all levels, on the basis of giving full play to the role of the CPPCC's political consultation in the "political consultation, democratic oversight, and participation in the deliberation and administration of state affairs" and other "party systems", have also strengthened and expanded the CPPCC's role of "social consultation". By giving play to the role of the People's Political Consultative Conference, dialogue, communication and consultation between related subjects in the process of social governance have been pushed forward and a governance in which non-governmental actors provide assistance has been enhanced.

Third, efforts have been made to strengthen the role of social governance of social organizations such as labor unions, youth leagues and women's federations. Since the 18th CPC National Congress, their roles have been greatly changed. As the means of political participation and expression of people's interests, they have fully performed their functions. As for the social organizations, many civil organizations and groups and Farmer Associations have been set up, playing their role in social governance. Social harmony and stability have been improved.

Fourth, the role of China's urban and rural autonomous organizations at the community level as a stabilizer in social governance has been given full play. They play an important role of making the society stable in social governance. Urban community residents' committees basically established residents' representative assemblies and consultation and deliberation committees, set up homeowners' committees, and urban grassroots democratic forms such as residents' councils and community hearings have strengthened grassroots social governance, with good results. In rural areas, villagers' committees have basically established the villagers' assemblies or the villagers' congresses to decide the important rural affairs in a democratic way. The rural villagers' committee has also established villager financial management groups and village affair supervision teams, which aim at carrying out such activities as the transparency of village affairs and democratic appraisal to strengthen the rural social governance and maintain rural social stability. Through elections, decision-making, governance and supervision, etc., in their communities and villages, the public of the Chinese people in urban and rural areas have directly played a democratic role in China's primary urban and rural social governance, which enhanced the effect of social collaboration.

4. Public participation has been advanced

In China, the public participation in the process of social governance refers to social organizations or ordinary individuals exclusive of government directly or indirectly participating in social governance through a variety of formal or informal ways to promote the benign development of social governance. Since the 18th CPC National Congress public participation in social governance has gradually been institutionalized. In social governance, public authoritative organizations are not only involved in social governance legislation, decision-making of public affairs, and strengthening the public governance, but also obtain information and take advice from social organizations or individuals with an open approach to realize the public participation in both social governance and public decision-making. The opinions from social organizations or individuals have been fully expressed. Public participation in the social governance has realized coordination and co-governance in the process of social governance.

Public participation should be actively expanded. We should adhere to the "putting people at the center", further broaden the channels for people's participation in social governance and legally safeguard people's right to access information, the right to participate, the right to make suggestions, the right to supervise. We have inherited and carried forward the good tradition of combining the efforts of both professionals and the public, given full play to the exemplary roles of the Party members and the Communist Youth League members, and deepened the reform of the militia reserve system. In addition, the specializing, professionalizing and socializing the peace-keeping volunteer forces, community workers and the teams of mass prevention and mass treatment have been developed and strengthened, and new mechanisms and new patterns of mass prevention and mass treatment under the new situation have been successfully developed. We give full play to the functions of traditional media and new media. By taking the popular publicity and education forms that people are delighted to hear and see, we mobilize and organize the public to care about, support and participate in social governance, thus promoting the social communication and coordination ability under the new media era.

The "Villagers Speak Out" system in Ningbo City, Zhejiang Province is a good refection of the reality of the public participation in grassroots rural social governance. Jiexia village in Xizhou Town, Xiangshan County, Ningbo City is a beautiful village surrounded by mountains on three sides and is the birthplace of the earliest local practice of "Villagers Speak Out". In 2009, the village received more than 10 million yuan (RMB) in compensation for the Baixi Reservoir diversion project, which became the fuse for the "Villagers Speak Out" practice. This money has led to many problems and conflicts in the village. Some people thought that "village cadres must have embezzled the compensation money", while other thought that "the subsidy funds are not evenly distributed" and so on. Along with this came the villagers' extreme distrust of village cadres, who were unwilling to listen and believe in what they said. Faced with this situation, the then village Party branch secretary Zheng Zufa was heartbroken, prompting the village Party branch and the village committee to make up their minds to let the villagers discuss and decide this matter. Thus, "villagers speak up" was born.

"Villagers speak out" concretely refers to the establishment of rooms villagers' speaking room, which is fixed for 1 to 2 speaking days per month, and the village Party branch (Party committee) presides over a speaking meeting to guide the villagers to rationally express their interest demands. Participants in the speech meeting include villagers who apply for speech, members of the village "two committees", members of the village board of supervisors, villagers' representatives, village veteran cadres, veteran party members, joint village cadres, etc. The range of affairs involves important and difficult issues in rural economic development and social stability as well as urgent and miscellaneous affairs related to the vital interests of the masses. The concrete procedure of villagers' speaking out consists of four sequences: "announcement - application - preparation - speaking out". First, in a timely manner before the meeting all the villagers are informed of the meeting time. Then those villagers who have the intention can make application to the village cadres which can propose changes and demand full reconsideration of the past decisions. Finally, the meeting is convened for the discussion. The villagers' opinions and suggestions are voiced. Everything in the meeting must be recorded, so as to make sure that everything has a record and can be tracked down.

Around the year 2009, as China continuously advanced the building of a moderately prosperous society in all respects, a series of new problems and conflicts arose in the vast rural grassroots due to the in-depth political, economic, cultural and social development and changes. solving these problems and resolving the resulting new conflicts in rural areas was an important issue that needed to be faced in China's rural grassroots social governance at that time. Xiangshan County of Ningbo City was good at summarizing the grassroots practices, bold in experimentation and innovation, and constantly summarizing "Villagers Speak Out" appearing in its jurisdiction, the new rural social governance model, which is actively participated by the majority of farmers, thus forming a "Villagers Speak Out" system with national influence. Later, based on this system, especially after the 18th National Congress of the Communist Party of China, the "four steps of harmonizing the village and benefiting the people" with the purpose of "harmonizing the village and benefiting the residents" has gradually taken shape, being implemented in the whole county, affecting the whole city, driving the whole province and lighting up the whole country.

5. Rule of law guarantees have been promoted

The rule of law guarantees in the process of the governance of the Chinese society refer to strengthening the social governance with the rule of law as the guarantee and making social governance become good governance and legal governance. Rule of law guarantees require all kinds of subjects the governance of the Chinese society respect the spirit of rule of law, follow the logic the legal system and abide by the laws and regulations. In October 2014, the *CCP Central Committee Decision concerning Several Major Issues in Comprehensively Advancing Governance According to Law* (hereafter: *Decision*) which was passed by the Fourth Plenary Session of the 18th CPC Central Committee made a comprehensive deployment on relying on rule of law guarantees in the governance of the Chinese society. On advancing the construction of a rule of law society, the *Decision* points out: "The people's rights and interests must rely on legal guarantees, the authority of the law must rely on the people upholding it." The governance of the Chinese society strengthens the leading role of the spirit of rule of law, and enhances the regulatory role of the Constitution and laws, which greatly raised the rule of law level of the governance of the Chinese society.

Since the Fourth Plenary Session of the 18th CPC Central Committee, the rule of law guarantees have played an important role in social governance and have produced a good effect in social governance.

Using legal means to solve the salient problems of social governance. Giving play to the guiding, normative, protective and disciplinary role of the rule of law, it has been accomplished to resolve social conflicts according to law, to prevent and combat crimes according to law, to standardize the social order according to law and to maintain social stability according to law. Revolving around the practical needs of strengthening the construction of social governance mechanism, we have promoted legislation, amendment, abolishment and interpretation of the related laws as well as making and improvement of related policies. We also have improved the means to maintain the lawful rights and interests of citizens and legal persons. The infringement cases are prevented from the source. By adhering to law-based administration, we have strengthened grassroots law-enforcement in some key fields such as food and drug administration, safety production, environmental protection, cultural market and network security, intensified the cohesion between administrative and criminal law enforcement and solved with great efforts the highlighted problems that the public raised. The reform of the judicial system has been deepened, the construction of a fair, efficient and authoritative judicial system sped up and the quality of case handing improved. The criminal policy of tempering justice with leniency has been carrying out. We crack down on a tiny minority of serious criminals in accordance with the law and at the same time minimize the social confrontation, trying to turn negative factors into positive ones. The publicity and education work on the rule of law have been strengthened and improved and the pertinence and effectiveness of law ruling publicity and education have been paid great attention to. We have promoted the whole society to establish the awareness of the rule of law, strengthened all the people's concept of the rule of law and urged all the people to respect and abide by the laws, led the officials and the public to take the laws as the basic principles to guide and standardize their behaviors, gradually forming the favorable law-ruling environment in which people handle affairs according to the laws, ask for legal help when confronted with problems, solve the problems by employing the laws and resolve conflicts by relying on the laws.

Law-based governance in the process of the governance of the Chinese society, governance has protected the people's rights endowed by the law. First of all, relying on rule of law guarantees, the Chinese people's freedom of movement has been guaranteed. Since the beginning of the new century, especially the 18th CPC National Congress, the scale of social population moving is quite huge. The Spring Festival travel rush of 2019 witnessed a total passenger flow of 2.99 billion. Second, relying on rule of law guarantees, the Chinese people's right to be informed has been guaranteed. According to provision of law, Chinese citizens have the right to participate in and the right to oversee public affairs. The premise of implementing these two rights is that the citizens enjoy the right to know. In the process of social governance in recent years, China has promoted the transparency of political activities, and strengthened the openness of government affairs at all levels and increased the protection of citizens' right to be informed. Third, in the process of social governance, by giving the full play to legal guarantees, China has done better in protecting the citizens' rights to develop, the right to subsistence, the right to vote, the right to be elected and other civil rights.

II. Building the basic public services system

In the process of social governance in China, basic public services guarantee all the residents' basic necessity of existence and development under the leadership of the government and it is also in line with economic social development. The basic public services system refers to the systematic and holistic institutional arrangement which consists of the scope and standards, the allocation of resources, management and operation, mode of supply as well as performance evaluation of basic public services. Since the 18th CPC National Congress, the governance of the Chinese society has strengthened the construction of the basic public services system, and a public services system with unique Chinese characteristics has taken shape. China's basic public services system mainly includes the following four aspects:

1. The main scope of the basic public services system has been established

The basic public services system in the governance of the Chinese society mainly includes the following eight areas: public education, labor-employment-entrepreneurship, social insurance, health care, social services, housing security, public culture and sports, services for the disabled. These eight areas focus are subdivided into more than 80 items. Each item has specified its service target, guiding standards of services, expenditure responsibility, and leading unit in charge, etc. The scope of the basic public services system in the governance of the Chinese society starts with solving the most direct and actual interests and problems that the people are most concerned about, enhancing the government' responsibilities, increasing the supply of public services, improving the joint construction capacity and sharing level of public services.

2. The list system of basic public services system has been established

In the governance of the Chinese society the list system of the public services system has been basically established. In January 2017, the State Council has issued the *Thirteenth Five-Year Plan for Promoting Equalization of Basic Public Services,* in which Annex 1 specifies the *Thirteenth Five-Year National List of Basic Public Services.* The list system of the basic public services system in the governance of the Chinese society has thus been established.

The elders in one Home for Seniors in Nantong, Jiangxi are exercising on the fitness equipment.

In the "list", service target refers to the target audience of each item, guiding standards of services refer to the guarantee level, coverage, realization degree, etc. of each item, expenditure responsibility refers to the fund-raising subjects of each item and their responsibilities, leading unit in charge refers to the main unit in charge at the national level, the concrete implementation is the responsibility of the local people's governments at all levels and relevant departments and units according to the division of responsibilities.

3. The basic direction of the basic public services system has been specified

The basic direction of the basic public services system in the governance of the Chinese society is based on the fundamental requirements of the social governance of "keeping the bottom line, developing as expected, co-ordinating resources, promoting equality, government taking responsibility, sharing the fruits of development, improving systems, reforming and innovating", finally achieving the goal that every child goes to school; every work is rewarded; the sick is treated; the elderly are taken good care of and everyone has a roof over the head. The basic direction of the basic public services system in the governance of the Chinese society mainly include equalization, universality, protection of people's basic needs, sustainability, etc. The equalization direction of the basic public services system in the governance of the Chinese society means that all the citizens can get roughly equal and fair access to basic public services, its core is promoting equality of opportunities, and its focus is ensuring people's opportunity to receive basic public services, rather than simple averaging.

4. Effective measures of the basic public services system have been implemented

First, equality and sharing are promoted. Poverty alleviation programs have been carried out with the focus on helping and supporting those in special difficulties. Full coverage program for permanent population in cities and towns has been promoted, the gap between urban and rural service narrowed, equalization of area service improved and the foundation of community service consolidated. When paying a visit to the economically poor people in Fuping County, Hebei Province to express his condolence, Xi Jinping pointed out that "the essential requirement of socialism is to eliminate poverty, improve people's wellbeing and achieve prosperity for all. To those who have difficulties in life, we will give them extra attention, extra care, extra love, trying our best to help them out. We put people's safety and their ordinary life in our minds and bringing warmth from our Party and government to every household."

Second, the service supply has been innovated. The classification reform of institutions has been sped up, the social forces participating in social governance have been guided, the development of voluntary and charitable services have been encouraged and the "Internet+" service benefiting people has been developed, etc.

Third, the resource guarantees have been strengthened. The financial security has been improved, talent team construction strengthened, the planning layout and land security enhanced and the standard service system established and perfected. What's more, support for the social credit system has been intensified.

Fourth, the planning implementation, supervision and assessment have been promoted. The obligations of relevant ministries under the State Council and people's governments below the province have been clearly defined. Performance assessment, supervision and accountability have been strengthened.

III. Basic formation of a modern social organization system

The 18th CPC National Congress pointed out that "we should accelerate the formation of the modern social organization system which is characterized by separating government administration from social community management, making rights and responsibility clear, and self-governing by law." In the *Decision of the CPC Central Committee on Some Major Issues concerning Comprehensively Deepening the Reform*, it is pointed out, "we should properly deal with the relationship between government and society, accelerate the construction of community system independent of government and promote social organizations to define their responsibilities, govern themselves by law and play their roles." Speeding up the formation of the modern system of social organization is very important for China to strengthen society building and social governance. Social organizations are one of the important subjects of the society building and social governance. The social organization system is about an autonomous social institution which is independent of the public power system and the social profit-making system in China. After the 18th CPC National Congress, China has gradually formed a more comprehensive social organization system. At present, China's modern social organization system has basically specified the relationship between the government and social organizations, and established the role of the social organizations as the subjects of social governance. In the process of the governance of the Chinese society, a modern system of social organization is formed which is characterized by the separation of community self-governance from government administration, well-defined power and responsibility, and governance by law.

China's social organizations can be roughly divided into intermediary agencies including legal firms, notarization institutions, accounting firms and assets appraisal departments, public-run non-enterprise units established by social forces in education, science and technology, culture, sanitation, sports and social welfare, other social organizations such as trade associations, institutes, chambers of commerce and foundations, etc. In China, such kind of social organizations belong to three categories, namely, public-run non-enterprise organs, social groups and foundations. Chinese social organizations roughly equal to the international "non-governmental organizations" or "non-profit organizations", etc. An important feature of China's social organization is autonomous management, self-organization, voluntary participation of the social organizations' members. Since the 18th CPC National Congress, in order to gradually form modern social organization system in the process of social governance, China makes the following efforts:

1. The separation of government and society has been strengthened

Since the 18th CPC National Congress, the Chinese government has attached great importance to the society building and social governance work. In the previous society building pattern in China, the government was dominant, giving orders and social organizations was submissive, taking orders passively. In order to push forward changes in this situation, the Chinese government has strengthened the work of dividing government and society, pushed forward the separation of government and social organizations, and made social organizations play a more important role in the process of the governance of the Chinese society. The following points in the strengthening of the separation of government and society have played a positive role in the formation of a modern system of social organization in China.

First, the social organization have been given the right to make the direct registration. To promote modern social governance and form a modern system of social organization, the Chinese government keeps adjusting the registration system of social organization and has implemented in many places direct registration by the management departments of Chinese social organization, achieving the goal of making social organizations independent of government and promoting social organizations' self-governance by law.

Second, the threshold for the social organization has been greatly lowered. Since the 18th CPC National Congress, China social organization management department has improved the social organization access system and reduced the requirements for social organizations to be recognized, creating a relaxed environment for the development of social organizations. In the process of social organization registration, the fees that the social organizations need to pay are reduced or exempted. The social organizations devoted to social welfare, voluntary services, public interests and charity have got substantial support, which has promoted the development of such kind of social organization.

Third, the government's control over social organizations has been changed. Since the 18ᵗʰ CPC National Congress, the Chinese government has strengthened the work to transform the functions of social organizations, and basically clarified the respective functions of the government and social organizations, which has laid a foundation for the work of dividing government administration and social organizations' self-management. The Chinese government has promoted the government and social organizations to clarify their respective responsibilities in the process of social governance. The detailed implementation of a large number of affairs about social governance and public service fall on the shoulders of social organizations. At the same time, the government has also given much support to social organizations in the form of funds for the purchase of public service and improved the enthusiasm of the social organizations. In this way the Chinese social governance has been strengthened. In addition, Chinese governments at all levels has transferred some micro-level public service functions to social organizations, such as business management function of some industries, the public service function of urban communities, serving function of rural production technology, social charity and social welfare function.

Fourth, the Chinese government has multiplied its purchases of social organization service. Since the 18ᵗʰ CPC National Congress, the Chinese government has increased its purchases of public service of social organizations to promote the division of government and social organizations and to accelerate the formation of modern social organization system. For this purpose, the Chinese government has made the catalogue of public services it needs to purchase, listed social organizations possessing the capability of providing public services and perfected the assessment criterion system of buying public services. Moreover, a financial supporting mechanism for the government to purchase public services has been set up, which has really improved the quality and effect of public service purchase. Beijing is at the forefront of the government's efforts to buy public services from social organizations.

In 2016, the Beijing Municipal Special Fund for Society Building will continue to purchase 500 service projects from different kinds of social organizations at all levels, totally 5 categories in 30 directions, covering social public services, social services for public interest, community services for public convenience, social governance services and decision-making and consultation services for society building. Through the way of government purchasing services, more social organizations are promoted to participate in social affairs; social organizations are cultivated and developed with an aim to set up an excellent model of social service, to promote the establishment of the modern social organization system, and ultimately improve and perfect the hub-like social organization system.

According to some statistics, since the establishment of the Beijing Municipal Special Fund for Society Building in 2010, a total investment of 420 million yuan has been made on purchasing 2,732 service projects of social organizations in total during 6 years in a row. Among these projects, 2,252 projects have been finished involving 43,500 social organizations, serving 17.63 million person-times, organizing 350,000 activities, providing 9.7 million hours' professional service and bringing relevant funds of 600 million yuan. "Red-candle Action", a project helping vulnerable children, "Family-friendly, Dream-realizing, developing together", a program providing comprehensive family service for women and children, the "Green Life-guard", a blue-sky rescue team, and "Passing Love" providing comfort for the special group of the elderly... such kind of service projects are gradually integrated into the life of Beijing residents. Those service projects from the social organizations are the fruits of supporting the service of social organizations in the form of purchasing services with the Beijing Municipal Special Fund for Society Building.[2]

2. The clarification of powers and responsibilities has been advanced

Making rights and responsibilities clear is the basic conditions of forming a modern social organization system. Since the 18th National Congress of CPC, the Chinese government has basically clarified the powers and responsibilities of the Chinese government itself and of Chinese social organizations and their management departments and operation guidance departments. The relationship of powers and responsibilities between the government and social organizations is defined clearly, and the role of the government and social organizations in the process of social governance is made clear, which has promoted the development of modern social organization system.

First, in order to make power and responsibility well defined, the Chinese government has made its own powers and its limits clear and strengthened

2   He Yong, Beijing Will Buy 500 Services from Social Organizations This Year, *People's Daily*, January 8, 2016, p. 6.

the self-construction of the management departments of the Chinese social organizations. Since the 18th National Congress of CPC, the Chinese government has strengthened the self-construction, accelerated the transformation into a service-oriented government for the satisfaction of the people and clarified the Chinese government's powers and its limits in social governance. At the same time, a standard coordinating and discussing agency for modern social organization work is gradually established to strengthen the self-construction of the Chinese social organization management departments. The Civil Affairs Ministry of the People's Republic of China is responsible for the overall planning, conducting, programming the work of national social organizations so as to coordinate and solve major issues of the development in the modern social organization system. Local Civil Affairs Departments at various levels have established regulatory institutions in order to coordinate the social organization registration. In addition, the Chinese government has strengthened the legislative work of modern social organization management, intensified law enforcement, increased the regulatory enforces, improved the relevant staff's professional quality and enhanced the authority of the Chinese social organization management departments.

Second, in order to make powers and responsibilities well defined, the Chinese government has promoted the establishment of the mechanism guiding social organizations' comprehensive business. Chinese social organization management department has strengthened by law its professional guidance, supervision and administration, and guided, regulated and supervised the activities of social organizations within the function scope conferred by the laws and regulations. The departments of finance, tax, banking, auditing, public security, human resources and social security of Chinese governments at all levels regulate and administrate the social organizations' activities of providing public services, participating in social governance, financial activities, social security in accordance with the law and monitor the illegal activities of social organizations. The departments of education, science and technology, culture, sanitation, sports, environmental protection and business, these different sectors of Chinese governments at all levels, incorporate social organizations into the industrial management and guide the social organization through making guidance policies and releasing information timely to promote the healthy development of social organizations.

Third, in order to distinguish powers from responsibility, the Chinese government has formulated the relevant policies for regulating social organizations. To make the duties of social organizations clear, the Chinese government has formulated a series of policies to standardize the internal operation mechanism such as social organizations' personnel system, professional ranking system, on-the-job training, financial regulations and social insurance etc., which has solved the practical difficulties of social organizations and their employees. In order to strengthen the supervision of social organizations, the Chinese government has also established the social organizations' evaluation index system characterized by openness, impartiality and fairness, and also constructed the Integrity Database and Public Reference Platform to Integrity Record. Chinese governments of all levels evaluate the running of social organizations regularly, objectively and fairly and announce the assessment results on time to guide governments of all levels to purchase the public services provided by social organizations.

3. Law-based self-governance has been implemented

Since the 18th CPC National Congress, under the guidance of the concept of "law-based self-governance", China's social organizations have taken the initiative to strengthen their construction and gradually upgraded to highly efficient, open and transparent, vibrant modern social organizations. An obvious feature of modern social organizations is their own perfect internal governance structure. Adhering to law-based self-governance, China's modern social organizations have continuously improved their governance structures, and enhanced their ability to provide public services. Meanwhile, China's modern social organizations have continually strengthened their independence and autonomy, improved their employee's basic qualities and basically realized self-management, self-restraint and self-development.

First, adhering to law-based self-governance, China's modern social organizations have continuously established and improved legal entity structures. China's modern social organizations have generally established and improved the legal entity charters of social organizations and established various rules and regulations for the operation and development of social organizations with the charters as the core. In terms of internal power operation mechanism, China's modern social organizations have basically established and improved the general assembly or representative assembly and formed normative systems for councils and boards of supervisors. Adhering to law-based self-governance, China's modern social organizations have strengthened the construction of internal democratic systems and have finally formed the democratic operation mechanism of democratic elections, democratic policy-making, democratic governance and democratic supervision.

Second, adhering to law-based self-governance, China's modern social organizations continually strengthen their capability of providing public services for the social governance. China's modern social organizations' main responsibility is to provide public services for China's social governance. Therefore, constantly improving their ability to provide public service for social governance is the top priority of their existence and development. Social organizations conduct self-management, which is targeted and feasible, increase their capacity of providing public service. Social organizations also strengthen their project management by taking the initiative to reduce the operating costs and improve fund utilizing efficiency, which has gradually expanded social influence and formed many competitive brand projects.

Third, adhering to law-based self-governance, China's modern social organizations have given full play to enthusiasm and initiative to provide public service. China's modern social organization are mainly set up spontaneously, which has high degree of autonomy, therefore adhere to law-based self-governance. On the basis of law-based self-governance, China's modern social organizations are independent of the Communist Party of China and China's government bodies. They have their own independence in business, personnel, finance and supplies. The independent operation pattern of social organizations has gradually improved the social organizations' enthusiasm and initiative to provide public services for China's social governance.

Fourth, adhering to law-based self-governance, China's modern social organizations have continuously improved the basic qualities of social organization practitioners. On the basis of law-based self-governance, China's modern social organizations have attached great importance to the cultivation of practitioners' basic qualities and the improvement of self-construction, which has enhanced the vitality of the social organizations. China's modern social organizations have established and improved the encouraging and constraining mechanisms within social organizations to improve the practitioners' working enthusiasm and initiative. In addition, social organizations have also gradually introduced accreditation systems on social practitioners' qualification, which has strengthened the professional evaluation of practitioners and formed teams of practitioners who are becoming more and more talented, specialized, professional and young and eventually promoted the development of China's modern social organizations.

IV. Innovating the social governance system

The innovation of social governance mechanism is an important part of constructing social governance system with Chinese characteristics. It is pointed out in the report of the 18th CPC National Congress that "we should speed up establishing a social governance mechanism integrating the management of source, dynamic management and emergency disposal", which is the theoretical basis of mechanism innovation for Chinese social governance. By correctly handling the relationship between governance administration and social autonomy, the Chinese government builds the modern system of social governance, continuously improves the public security mechanism under the rule of law and the comprehensive governance and establishes social development system aiming at equalization of public services. When attending Shanghai delegation's deliberation in the Second Session of the 12th National People's Congress, Xi Jinping pointed out: "To strengthen and innovate social governance, we should put the focus on system innovation with people in the center. Only when people are living in harmony, the society will be stable. The focus of social governance is on urban and rural communities. When the community service and management is competent, the foundation of social governance is solid. We have to make a thorough investigation and research of the governance system, deepening and expanding the grid of management, and transferring resources, service and management to the primary level as far as possible to make the community public have responsibilities, rights and resources in hand so as to provide effective service and management. We should strengthen the urban normalized management by focusing on the prominent problems that the public raise repeatedly and vigorously dealing with persistent ailments in urban management. We should strengthen the population service management, mobilizing market-based and law-based approaches to promote the orderly flow of population, control the total population, and optimize the population structure." The philosophy of social governance put forward by Xi Jinping has important theoretical and practical significance in the history of society building in China. To strengthen social governance, we have to innovate the philosophy of social governance, strengthen dynamic social management, improve social emergency management, systematically and comprehensively promote society building and social governance and form a complete and reasonable social governance mechanism.

1. The concept of social governance has been innovated

The most important thing to innovate social governance mechanism is to innovate the concept of social governance. Since the 18th CPC National Congress, China has strengthened the innovation of the concept of social governance in the process of promoting the social governance. It is pointed out in the *Decision of the CPC Central Committee on Some Major Issues Concerning Comprehensively Deepening the Reform* that "we should adhere to law-based governance, strengthen rule of law guarantees, use rule of law thinking and rule of law methods to resolve social conflicts. Persist in comprehensive governance, strengthen moral restraint, standardize social actions, moderate relationships of interests, coordinate social relationships and resolve social problems. Persist in governing from the source, dealing with both symptoms and root causes, focus on dealing with the roots, make networked management and socialized management into the direction, complete comprehensive grass roots service management platforms, timely reflect and coordinate the interests and appeals of the popular masses in all areas and at all levels." Xi Jinping pointed out: "There is only the difference of a word in Chinese between governance and management, but it reflects the systematic governance, law-based governance, governance at the source and comprehensive implementation of policies. Social governance is a scientific undertaking which improves the quality of officials, takes the training of a group of specialized officials in city management as the top task, construct and manage cities with scientific attitude, advanced philosophy and professional knowledge."[3] As a result, the innovation of the concept of social governance has gradually taken shape in China. China's new concept of strengthening social governance lies in adhering to systematic governance, law-based governance, comprehensive governance and governance at the source.

First, adhere to the concept of systematic governance. In the era of social management, the Chinese government played a leading role in the whole society building process. After the 18th CPC National Congress, society building in China has been pushed from the era of social management into a new era of social governance. In the era of social governance, about the

---

3 Promote the Construction of Pilot Free Trade Zone in Shanghai China, Strengthen and Innovate the Social Governance of the Megacities, *People's Daily*. March 6, 2014, p. 1.

positioning of government, one important aspect is that the government bears principal responsibility in the whole process of social governance. At the same time, in the process of social governance in this new era, emphasis is placed on strengthening conceptual innovation and the concept of systematic social governance has gradually taken shape. In the process of social governance, the government takes the major responsibility and at the same time mobilizes social organizations, individual citizens and so on to forms a pattern of multiple social subjects participating in the systematic governance. In the process of social governance, the Chinese government adheres to the concept of systematic governance, which gives full play to its own initiative and at the same time arouses the enthusiasm of other subjects such as social organizations and individual citizens, forming a social governance pattern of coordination and co-governance.

Second, adhere to the concept of law-based governance. The Fourth Plenary Session of the 18th CPC Central Committee pointed out: "We will strengthen the entire population's rule of law consciousness, move the construction of a rule of law society forward." The construction of a rule of law society needs to establish the concept of law-based governance. In the process of promoting social governance, China has improved social governance mechanism, innovated approaches of social governance and formed the concept of law-based governance, which has gradually realized the promotion and reinforcement of social governance in accordance with law.

Third, adhere to the concept of comprehensive governance. In the process of promoting social governance, the Chinese government has strengthened the concept of comprehensive governance. Under the guidance of the concept of comprehensive governance, Chinese social governance has gradually shifted from mainly relying on a single administrative means to mobilizing comprehensively a variety of approaches. The means employed in the governance of the Chinese society include means of mediating social conflicts, methods of self-discipline in regulating behaviors and measures of restraining in moral education, etc. The comprehensive application of those methods has produced a good effect in social governance.

Fourth, adhere to the concept of governance at the source. The innovation of the social governance by China strengthens the shift to governance at the source. In the process of advancing social governance, China has transformed its practice from treatment after the event to preparation in advance and development during the process, making efforts to strengthen social governance from the source and from the beginning. During the process, the Chinese government has innovated and gradually formed the concept of governance at the source. On the one hand, governance at the source is reflected in the government's decision-making. The government listens to the public, makes full argumentation and organizes necessary hearings to make sure that the decisions made conform to the reality, meet the demands of the public and accord with national conditions and national strength. On the other hand, governance at the source is embodied in the fact that the Chinese governments at all levels actively promote the practice of relying on public self-governance and community work to solve various kinds of interest demands in the process of social governance to decrease and solve interest conflicts, build up social harmony and stimulate social vitality.

2. Social dynamics governance has been strengthened

Innovating the social governance mechanism has a starting line but no finishing line. Innovating social governance requires to continuously improve the level of social governance to promote social stability and orderliness and ensure that the people live and work in peace and contentment. Innovating social governance requires to continuously strengthen coordination of the dynamics and pay more attention to the equal communication and consultation and timely resolving social conflicts. All kinds of problems arising in the process of social governance should be solved by using innovative methods; all kinds of phenomena in the process of social governance should be treated by using the "point of view of movement"; the social governance should be strengthened by using dynamic ways. Xi Jinping pointed out: "The innovation of social governance must center on the fundamental interests of the public and start from the direct realistic issues concerning people's interests that the public cares most. Now, there exist many problems in the community-level systems of social governance, which must be settled through reform. Urban and rural communities are recognized as the 'the last kilometer' connecting the Party and the public. We should take strengthening the construction of the Party at the community level and consolidating the Party's ruling as a guideline for social governance and primary construction to expand further the regional construction of the Party. We will adjust and improve unsuitable management system and mechanism, move the center of management to lower levels, decentralizing the central government's administration by giving the regular specific services and management responsibility to communities at different levels, distributing human resources, fund, materials, and rights, responsibility and profits to primary organizations and handing over the resources and strength serving the people to community-level organizations which are closest to the public to strengthen primary organizations' influence and appeal."[4] Strengthening social dynamics governance and optimizing institutional setting, we have straightened out the governance mechanism of social services, specified and innovated social governance, promoted the transformation of social governance functions, improved the management of services for the moving population and strengthened the improvement of the people's wellbeing, paying close attention to and attaching importance to the people's wellbeing, safeguarding and improving people's wellbeing so as to make fruits of social governance benefit more people in China. Strengthening social dynamics governance should start from the following three aspects:

First, we should attach importance to prevent and resolve social conflicts from the source. The starting point of preventing and resolving social conflicts lies in adhering to "putting people at the center" and strengthening the prevention of the occurrence of social conflicts from the source. Once social conflicts fail to be prevented at the source, we should move to the stage of resolving social conflicts in time to prevent the expansion of social conflicts, try to resolve social conflicts at the initial stage, and try to prevent the intensification of social conflicts. Social dynamics governance is to closely follow each stage of the emergence, development, change and intensification of social conflicts, treat the movement and change of social conflicts with dynamic methods, try to eliminate social conflicts in the bud and effectively avoid the intensification of social conflicts. If we take the lead again, we should try our best to strengthen the predictive prevention of social conflicts, increase the construction of social governance mechanism to avoid social conflicts, and form a harmonious and stable state of good governance. The key to strengthening social dynamics governance lies in innovation, its core lies in paying attention to and attaching importance to

---

4 The Party Literature Research Office of the CPC Central Committee, *Excerpts from Xi Jinping's Treatises on Building a Moderately Prosperous Society in All Respects*, Central Party Literature Press, 2016, p. 148.

the people's interests, and earnestly "putting people at the center". Social dynamics governance is a regular, basic and fundamental work, and requires to dynamically, daily and timely track the governance proceeding from the people's interests so that social governance is in a harmonious and orderly state in and the stability of social life is maintained.

Second, we will mobilize the enthusiasm of all walks of life to form a conjoined force in social governance. Compared with social management, social governance is characterized by its multiplicity in agency. The subject of social governance is multiple, while the subject of social management is unitary. In social governance, we adhere to the systematic governance, which has mobilized the enthusiasm of the public and organizations in all fields and formed a powerful force of social governance. Therefore, the level of the social governance has been increased. Systematic social governance requires that we strengthen the leadership of the Party Committee, give full play to the government's leading role, encourage and support the participation of the various social forces in the social governance to form a powerful conjoined force of social governance, finally realize the good interaction among government governance, social self-adjustment and residents' autonomy and reach an ideal state of co-governance, coordinated separated governance and co-working of central governance and separated governance.

Third, we should continuously raise the rule of law level of the social governance by strengthening the rule of law consciousness. Strengthening social dynamics governance requires attaching great importance to and strengthening the concept of rule of law and using rule of law approach to resolve social conflicts in the process of social governance. We should raise the rule of law consciousness and raise the rule of law level of the social governance from the perspective of ruling the country in accordance with law, building a rule of law country and building a rule of law society. In the process social dynamics governance, the authoritative position of law in resolving social conflicts, use law to maintain social fairness and justice, and make people accustomed to using law to solve problems related to their own interests. To prevent and resolve social conflicts in the process of social governance, we should also rely on the rule of law. Adherence to the organic combination of rule of law education and rule of law practice and carrying out social governance activities according to law has raised the rule of law level of social governance.

3. Social emergency governance has been perfected

Improving social emergency governance is an important aspect of the innovation of the social governance mechanism. Since the 18th CPC National Congress, the Chinese government has strengthened the social emergency governance, effectively responded to and properly handled unexpected public incidents, eliminated the negative factors and stimulated the social vitality, maximally promoting social harmony. We have carried out a pilot innovation of synthesizing social governance, adhering to the coordination of separate parts, strengthened the integration of community social governance, serving ability and service resources, promoted the network of social governance and improved the level of social emergency governance.

First, elevating the concept of social emergency governance. Conception is the precursor of action, and consensus is the prime mover of practice. In recent years, the capacity and level of emergency governance work of the Chinese government has been greatly improved. The reason for this is that the Chinese government has attached great importance to and effectively improved the concept of social emergency governance. "Putting people at the center" is the core of social emergency governance. If we strengthen the concept of social emergency governance with the people in mind, we can try our best to achieve no trouble, less trouble and no big trouble in the process of actual social governance. Xi Jinping pointed out: "Human lives are vital, and development must not be at the expense of human life as the price. This must be a red line that cannot be crossed."[5] In the process of social emergency governance, the red line consciousness has become an important bottom line, which has been highlighted in the concept of social emergency governance. In the process of social governance, the Chinese government continuously reinforces "putting people at the center", adheres to the idea that life is the top priority and strengthens the principle of relying on the people and working for the people. Therefore, the work of social emergency governance has reached the goal of adhering to the bottom line and preparing for dangers while living in peace. Social emergency governance has been added to the list of the routine work and emergency preparing and emergency planning have been made, which have improved the level of social emergency governance.

---

5   Always Put the Safety of People's Lives in the First Place and Effectively Prevent the Occurrence of Serious Production Accidents, *People's Daily*, June 8, 2013, p. 1.

Second, the mechanism of social emergency governance has been perfected. In recent years, the Chinese government has been constantly summing up the experience and lessons learned from dealing with all kinds of emergencies and has come up with a set of effective mechanisms of social emergency governance after gradual exploration, which have been improved in the constant and repeated applications. In the social emergency governance mechanism, an emergency is divided in four stages: before the event, incidence, during the event and after the stage after the event and corresponding measures are taken according to different features of each stage. According to the characteristics of each period, the social emergency governance mechanism mainly includes seven aspects, namely, the mechanism of precaution and preparation, the mechanism of monitoring and warning, information reporting mechanism, emergency handling mechanism, the restoration and reconstruction mechanism, the public opinion guidance mechanism, and the investigation and evaluation mechanism. In face of a specific emergency, departments of the Central government and local governments perform their duties, cooperate with each other, and jointly formed the social emergency governance mechanism which operates effectively.

Third, the protection capacity of the social emergency governance has been enhanced. The protection capacity of China's social emergency governance, namely the rescuing and handling capacity in emergency is mainly embodied in the rescuing and handling power, emergency supplies and equipment preparation and emergency transportation and communication and other protection capacities in emergency. The Chinese government has basically formed the social emergency governance team system with professional teams as the basic force, the public security armed police and the people's army as the assault force, and expert teams, part-time teams of enterprises and institutions, and volunteer teams as auxiliary forces. China has initially established a four-level linkage social emergency governance protection network system at the national, provincial, municipal and county levels for responding to various emergencies at any time. China has effectively enhanced the protection capacity of the social emergency governance.

Chapter Five

Strengthening and Innovating
Social Governance

Since the 18th CPC National Congress, Chinese government has adhered to the ruling philosophy of "putting the people at the center" and adhered to strengthening society building and innovating social governance. The Third Plenary Session of the 18th CPC Central Committee pointed out: "To make innovations in social governance, we must direct our primary attention to safeguarding the fundamental interests of the broadest masses of the people, increase the factors of harmony to the maximum, invigorate social development and improve the social governance level, safeguard national security, ensure that the people live and work in peace and contentment, and that the society is stable and orderly." Therefore, in recent years, the Chinese government has vigorously advanced the society building, focused on strengthening and innovating social governance, attached great importance to safeguarding and improving people's wellbeing, and prompted the fruits of reform and development to benefit all people in a greater and fairer way. As Xi Jinping pointed out: "We will continue strengthening and innovating social governance, improve the social governance system of socialism with Chinese characteristics and strive to build a higher level of peaceful China, and further enhance the people's sense of security." To strengthen and innovate social governance, Chinese government has improved the mechanism of preventing and resolving social conflicts, innovated and perfected the social credit system, established and improved the public safety system and established and consolidated the national security system.

I. Perfecting the system for preventing and resolving social conflicts

Contradictions exist everywhere. There are contradictions in each thing. Contradictions run through the whole process of development of things. That is to say, contradictions are present everywhere and at all times. Contradictions are the driving force for the things to develop. It's normal that contradictions exist in the social field. It is impossible to find a society where there is no contradiction. Improving the system of preventing and resolving social conflicts is a crucial part for the society to reduce the disharmonious factors, transform negative factors into positive factors, stimulate the creativity of society and promote social stability and orderliness. Hence, only by actively facing social conflicts and effectively preventing and resolving conflicts, can we better advance social progress and improve social governance. In his report to the 19th CPC National Congress, Xi Jinping pointed out that "we should continue the construction of the system of preventing and resolving social conflicts and handle contradictions among our people in a proper way". In recent years, Chinese government has improved the mechanism of evaluating risks to social stability, established and improved the system for preventing and resolving social conflicts, advanced the construction of a rule of law society, and enhanced social harmony and stability.

1. Mechanisms to assess risks to social stability have been improved

Since the 18th CPC National Congress, the Chinese government has attached great importance to building mechanisms for assessing risks to social stability. *Decision of the CPC Central Committee on Some Major Issues Concerning Comprehensively Deepening the Reform* passed at the Third Plenary Session of the 18th CPC Central Committee emphasized "innovating systems that can effectively prevent and solve social conflicts. We will improve social stability risk assessment mechanism for major policy decisions. We will establish an open and orderly mechanism under which people can express their grievances, psychological intervention is conducted, conflicts are mediated and rights and interests are guaranteed, so as to ensure that the problems of the people can be reported, conflicts can be resolved and the people's rights and interests can be guaranteed." In order to prevent and resolve social conflicts to the greatest extent, an assessment of the potential risks to social stability made before making major decisions which concern people's interests so as to solve problems and contradictions that may affect people's interests and social stability before major decisions are made. As for those vital decisions, key projects and major programs concerning people's wellbeing and social stability, public displays and hearings should be held before they are introduced formally to listen to people's advice in order to take into account possible social risks, environment impact, contradictions, disputes and various kinds of destabilizing elements. In this way, potential or lurking problems may be revealed and solved in a timely manner to ensure that the decisions and legislations are legal, rational, feasible and safe. Meanwhile, during the process of conducting social governance and providing services, Chinese civil administration departments put wide social participation and democratic discussion and argumentation into practice when making policies, plans or decisions to make the policies, plans and decisions that are made conform to the reality of society building and meet people's reasonable demands.

2. Mechanisms to prevent and resolve social conflicts have been established

Establishing an effective mechanism of preventing and resolving social conflicts is the key part of strengthening and innovating social governance. In his speech at the 14th group study session of the Political Bureau of the 18th CPC Central Committee, Xi Jinping emphasized: "To safeguard national security we must maintain social harmony and stability, prevent and resolve social conflicts, and improve our institutions, mechanisms, policies and practical endeavors to make this happen. We should make China's development more comprehensive, coordinated and sustainable, work harder to safeguard and improve the people's well-being, and tackle social conflicts at the source. We should make promoting social fairness, justice and the people's well-being our ultimate goal, and increase our efforts in balancing the interests of all sectors, so that all the people can increasingly share in the fruits of development in a fairer way. We should implement and improve the institutions and mechanisms for protecting the legitimate rights and interests of the people, and the mechanism for assessing potential risks, so as to reduce and prevent conflicts of interest. We should comprehensively promote law-based governance, and better safeguard the people's legitimate rights and interests. We should encourage all the people to resolve all social conflicts through legal procedures and by legal means, and ensure that people do things according to law, examine the law provisions in case of conflict, and use laws to solve problems and conflicts." To establish a mechanism of effectively preventing and resolving social conflicts, we should pay attention to establishing a smooth and orderly mechanism for people to express their demands, setting up a mechanism of effective psychological intervention and building a practical conflict-mediating mechanism and a mechanism of safeguarding people's rights and interests.

First, the smooth and ordered appeal-expressing mechanism has been perfected. We have improved the institutional platform which is conducive for the interest subjects to express their interest appeals and makes the channels accessible and smooth through which interest subjects can voice and report their demands. We have improved the system of public opinion survey, information disclosure system, hearing system, consultation and negotiation system and referendum system. We have improved improve the appeal-expressing mechanisms of litigation, arbitration and administrative reconsideration. What's more, we have further freed the social benefit expressing function of People's Congresses, of the leading committees of the Chinese People's Political Consultative Conference (CPPCC), people's mass organizations, social organizations, self-government organizations at the community level, news media and via Internet, thus broadened the channels for the free expression of people's appeals and petitions. We have improved the system of petition letters and telephone calls for complaints and also improved the mechanism of conveying these petitions letters and complaints to legal bodies so that they are dealt lawfully.

Second, effective mechanisms of psychological aid were established. The establishment of psychological aid system can help individuals in crisis receive psychological aid in a timely manner, get out of psychological crisis as soon as possible thus return to normal state of mind. By establishing psychological crisis intervention-aid and warning system, we can prevent and reduce social risks and social conflicts caused by people in psychological disorder so as to effectively prevent and resolve such social conflicts and risks.

Third, the contradiction mediation mechanisms have been strengthened. The system of people's mediation, administrative mediation and judicial mediation working together has been reinforced. We have built an integrated treatment mechanism for mediating and resolving social conflicts and disputes and formed the mode of coordinating work through an integrated mechanism to prevent and resolve social conflicts, which has enhanced the effectiveness of preventing and resolving social conflicts.

Fourth, the system of safeguarding people's rights and interests were improved. In order to safeguard and realize people's immediate interests, our efforts focus on resolving the issues of greatest concern to people, such as land expropriation, house demolition, enterprise restructuring, wages, education, health care, social security, environmental protection, production safety in the workplaces, food and drug safety and urban management. By establishing a sound social security mechanism, we have effectively safeguarded the legitimate rights and interests of the people.

3. The construction of a rule of law society has been advanced

Rule of law is the basic principle and method of the social governance. Advancing the rule of law concerning society building in all respects is an important action to realize the modernization of social governance. Since the 18th National Congress of CPC, the Chinese government has advanced the construction of a rule of law society in all respects, adhered to the rule of law concerning society building and social governance, strengthened law-based society building and social governance and resolved various social conflicts and problems appearing in the process of society building and social governance by using rule of law. By strengthening legislation, justice, law enforcement, compliance with the law and law-abiding and other links in all respects, we have effectively advanced the construction of a rule of law society and prevented and resolved social conflicts.

Firstly, the legislation processes in the social field have been sped up. We have exerted more efforts on legislation in normalizing social organizations, urban and rural communities and social securities, etc. While in an investigation tour in Fujian Province, Xi Jinping emphasized: "the community is small but connected to thousands of households. So, it is very important to implement community work well. Since the Party organizations, Party members and Party officials are in constant contact with the residents, they

On March, 27, 2017, "Bringing the Rule of Law to the Neighborhood by Organizing 100 Publicity Activities" was held in Congchuan District, Nantong City, Jiangsu Province. In this district, more publicity activities with rich content and diversified forms were organized in the neighborhoods to promote the rule of law.

should ponder about how to make people's life more affluent, how to speed up the process of handling affairs related to people's well-being, how to make the channel more expedite for people to appeal, how to make people feel safer and happier and how to make households enjoy the warmth of our Party and government." Recently the government has strengthened all sorts of legislation related to the social field, i.e., related to people in the urban and rural communities, it has effectively laid a legal foundation for the society building and social governance by establishing laws and regulations and promoted the construction of a rule of law society in China.

Secondly, systematic judicial reforms and law enforcement mechanisms have been established and improved. The new rule of law and judicial reforms have greatly improved the transparency of judicial procedures and law enforcement and exerted concrete efforts to ensure that the justice and law enforcement are strict, standardized, impartial and civilized, thus comprehensively developed the authoritative status of the rule of law in the whole society which can better safeguard people's rights and interests. Social fairness and justice have been promoted and the construction of a rule of law society has been advanced. Based on the rule of law, legal legislation and effective legal procedures, we have ensured that the society building and social governance is permeated by the notion of the rule of law, established the authority of the laws and promoted the establishment judicial organizations so as to prevent and resolve social conflicts by means of legal means and law enforcement.

Thirdly, the rule of law notion and rule of law consciousness of the entire society has been strengthened. In-depth publicity and education on the rule of law society has been carried out, enabling numerous cadres and people to "learn the law, know the law, comply with the law, use the law and abide by the law", establishing the basic belief in the supremacy of the law and the code of conduct in the whole society, strengthening the notion of the rule of law in the whole society and raising the level of of rule of law consciousness of the whole society. The fundamental work of carrying out social governance in accordance with law has been strengthened, a social governance pattern jointly built and shared by the whole people has been built, the capacity and level of governing the society in accordance with law have been raised. We have achieved that the whole society is both full of vitality and harmonious, stable and orderly and achieved remarkable results in the construction of a rule of law society.

II. Innovating and perfecting the social credit system

A perfect social credit system is an important hall mark of a mature socialist market economy and the full-fledged law system is the foundation of the social credit system, and a powerful government supervision system is an important political guarantee for the social credit system to operate. The 18th CPC National Congress pointed that "we must strengthen the construction of government administrative credibility, business trust, social credibility and judicial integrity". The *Decision of the CPC Central Committee on Some Major Issues Concerning Comprehensively Deepening the Reform* passed at the Third Plenary Session of the 18th CPC Central Committee emphasized "to establish and improve a social credit system, to commend honesty and punish dishonesty." In July 2014, the State Council issued the *Planning Outline for the Construction of A Social Credit System (2014-2020)* and put forward the overall idea and basic principles of constructing a social credit system. The *13th Five-Year Plan for Economic and Social Development of the People's Republic of China* proposed to "perfect the social credit system" and "speed up the construction of credibility in key fields such as government administrative credibility, business trust, social credibility and judicial integrity, to advance credit information sharing and perfect the mechanisms of encouraging and punishing so as to improve the level of integrity of the whole society." Therefore, the construction of Chinese social credit system mainly includes advancing constructing government administrative credibility, business trust, social credibility and judicial integrity, with emphasis on building a culture of integrity and establishing a mechanism to encourage keeping trust and punish breaking trust. Since the 18th National Congress of the Communist Party of China, the Chinese government has attached great importance to the construction of a social credit mechanism and adhered to "putting people at the center", which has formed a favorable atmosphere where it is an honor to keep trust and it is a shame to break trust. In this way, honesty and trustworthiness have become a basic consensus and a self-disciplined moral standard for all people. Meanwhile, it has also sped up and promoted the credit construction in such key fields as government administrative credibility, business trust, social credibility and judicial integrity. In order to innovate and improve social credit system, the Chinese government has perfected the management of credit information, strengthened credit information sharing, perfected the mechanism to encourage keeping trust and punish breaking trust and cultivated and standardized the credit servives market, which have raised the credibility level of the whole society.

1. The credit information management system has been improved

A unified social credit rating code system has been implemented nationwide. A nationwide unified credit information collection and management standard has been formulated. In accordance with the law, it has been ensured that management over the collection, sharing, usage, and release of credit information is based on the type of information, the protection of credit information involving personal privacy or business secrets has been strengthened. The development of legislation regarding credit has been moved forward faster. In terms of the construction of a sound credit information management system, the city of Guangzhou City, Guangdong Province, is ahead of the nation.

Guangzhou City, Guangdong Province has set up a credit platform which covers six credit subjects and uses unified credit rating code and has improved the credit information management system. In July 2014, the State Council printed and issued *Planning Outline for the Construction of A Social Credit System (2014-2020)* which clearly stated that after a unified social credit code was established, Guangzhou has been actively constructing "Public Credit Information Management Platform in Guangzhou" and adopted unified social credit rating code system which covers six subjects including government, judicial organs, enterprises, public institutions, social organizations and individuals.

Recently, the Guangzhou E-Government Administration Center has issued a bidding announcement that the government will bid to purchase two subprograms of the city's Public Credit Information Management System with a maximum price of 10.4 million RMB. This means Guangzhou strides one step forward to construct credit platform. According to the plan, Guangzhou's future credit system will build a powerful "three-dimensional web" covering six subjects including government, judicial organs, enterprises, public institutions, social organizations and individuals.

Guangzhou now is exerting great efforts to set up Public Credit Information Management System. It will build a unified social credit rating code to integrate and share the credit information scattered in various departments so as to form a credit system platform in the end. "From now on, every citizen and every institution will have an own social credit rating code which will record their credit information such as finance, tax and traffic violation," the person in charge of the relevant department said.

It is worth mentioning that Guangzhou government set up information platform with the government itself as the very beginning. Among the six credit subjects, "whether the government keeps its word" is ranked the first in the assessment, which aims to make the government leads and sets a model in the construction of social credit system to fully improve credibility level of the city Guangzhou.

More specifically, Guangzhou states that to push forward the construction of government administrative credibility, they will make more and more government administration information known to the public. Since 2015, Guangzhou government has posted all the government affairs online, achieving a goal of 100% publicity on the website. As for the government purchase and offer or transfer of the right to the use of the land, the government aims to have 80% of the trades in public resource handled with "one stop service" and the percentage is planned to amount to 100% in 2020.

Among these, civil servants' credibility becomes an important part of the government credibility. The goal of Guangzhou is that 100% of civil servants will have credit records in the year 2020, which will become a key criterion in the appraising, assessment, promotion, appointment, and model-selecting.

After the construction of the credit system, Guangzhou gradually enlarged the scope of information collection. In 2015, the public credit information database had been built which covers all the social legal persons. In 2020, a public credit information management System which is designed to cover the whole society will be built, among which the individual credit system undoubtedly is a big concern. According to some relevant organizations, the coverage of individual credit records is 60% in 2015 and will reach 90% in 2020.[1]

---

1   Credit Network: How to Balance Being Tight and Loose (A First Line Investigation) by He Linping, *People's Daily*, Feb 11, 2015, p. 6.

2. Joint construction and sharing of credit information has been improved

We have established an information-disclosure and credit-recording system and rapidly improved the credit records of all kinds of market subjects and social members. We have promoted the integration of sectoral, industrial and local credit information, established collection mechanisms of enterprise credit information, improved the sharing platform of national credit information and built the national enterprise credit information publicity system. In addition, we have promoted by law the opening and sharing of credit information resources of the whole society. The joint construction and sharing of credit information resources have boosted the development of the credit society and changed the daily life of the Chinese people. In recent years, with the advancing of joint construction and sharing of credit information, social credit is improving gradually and cashless life is becoming a part of the daily life of the Chinese people.

While the cashless life is gaining more and more popularity, credit is becoming a great treasure for everyone and has become a second identity of every person.

All basic necessities of life can be attained by an easy motion of swiping the mobile phone. Even when we want to have a Roujiamo (a Chinese hamburger or pancake stuffed with pork) at the roadside, we can just scan codes without any cash. The cashless life represented by Alipay was appraised not long ago as one of the "New Four Inventions" of China by the youths of the countries along "the Belt and Road Initiatives". As early as at the beginning of 2016, an American journalist came to Beijing to experience a 24-hour cashless life and was totally shocked by China's powerful and convenient online payment after a whole day's payment with WeChat.

Gradually and unconsciously, there are fewer and fewer occasions in our life when we have to use cash. Gradually and unconsciously, "You can pay through Alipay" has become an advertisement for the Chinese people when we travel abroad in our neighbor countries.

We can bicycle by credit, stay in a hotel by credit and receive medical treatment by credit and so on. What lies behind the cashless life is not only the change of people's methods of making payment but also the accumulation of credit through payments.

Deposit used to be a trading threshold for cashless life. However, under the wave of great economic growth, some service platforms such as bicycle sharing choose to cooperate with the personal credit system and eliminate the deposit requirement to lower the threshold for new users. Recently, shared bicycles can be rented or borrowed with credit and no deposit is required in Beijing and Shanghai, which not only saves time but also reduces the deposit risk.

In addition, it is becoming more and more popular that we can leave the car parking lots without making any payment, also we can first stay in hotel and then pay later, we can take a bus by just scanning our code in the smartphone and we can get a bank loan and pay back in installments, which shows that individual creditworthiness is becoming everyone's valuable fortune as well as the second identity with the popularization of cashless life. It may be difficult to live with the lack of credit or a bad credit record. The establishment of social credit system can promote the comprehensive development of society as a whole.[2]

The photo shows a crowded hall wherein people are trying to buy or book train tickets, those with high social credit scores can have some discount in prices or pay in a later time appropriate for them.

---

2   Cashless Life Has Come. Is the Credit Society Still Far Away? (On People's Wellbeing) by Mu Dong, *People's Daily*, June 22, 2017, p. 22.

3. Mechanisms to encourage keeping trust and punish breaking trust have been improved

We have established and improved the credit encouragement and discredit punishment mechanism. In market supervision and public service, we carry out incentive policies that honest and trustworthy persons are provided with facilitated and easier services. We have promoted the construction of credit supervision, warning and disciplinary system for those who default on their court orders, enhanced the judicial credit and advanced the construction of social credit system. We have established and perfected a coordinated response and a joint reprimand mechanism among different sections, regions and industries, strengthened the action of publicizing and supervising enterprises' creditworthiness in accordance with law. We have implemented a blacklisting system and a mechanism of market restrictions for those enterprises that have lost their creditworthiness. What's more, we have improved the ability of checking and controlling, improved the blacklisting system of those who default on their court orders and we have also perfected the working system that the Party and government organs support the People's Court in their executions. The construction of the credit discipline pattern that "Discredit Somewhere, Inaccessibility Everywhere" makes things somewhat difficult for those who have lost their creditworthiness. In terms of improving the system of encouraging credit and punishing discredit, the measures that has been taken in Nanhai district, Foshan City, Guangdong Province are properly and effectively implemented, which are worthy of learning and emulating. In Nanhai district, Foshan City, during the construction of social credit system, they have adhered to the combination of motivation and punishment. Thus, people or enterprises who keep their promises are promoted while those who break their promises may face obstacles everywhere, which bring into play the guiding and regulating role of the social credit system.

Nanhai District is dominated by small and medium-sized manufacturing enterprises and private individual economy. Its structural reform in supply focuses more on how to solve the problem that manufacturing enterprises move to a medium-to-high level of development, how to effectively address the problem of medium, small, and micro enterprises being unable to access loans or having to pay high interest to secure loans. Therefore, three banners of quality, credit and service are held in Nanhai District to promote the transformation and upgrading of enterprises, keep up with international standard and grasp more market power. They have promoted the transformation of financing mode of small and medium-sized enterprises from "mortgage oriented" to "credit oriented", reducing corporate financing costs, improving administration efficiency and lowering enterprise costs.

A chain of social credit reward and discredit punishment has been established. Nanhai District has sped up the construction of social credit system and built the chain of incentives and restraints with the focus on breaking the imbalance between finance and the real economy to strengthen financial support to the real economy and promote the transition of the society from regulation and constraint oriented to incentive and guide oriented so as to reduce the costs of economic development and social governance. They focused on the construction of credit registry cloud of "governments, banks and enterprises" and credit and finance innovation platforms in Nanhai District. They have built the effective mechanisms for jointly building and sharing information and steadily promoted the construction of "one network" in Nanhai District. They have strengthened the regional credit cooperation and built the comprehensive credit information center of Small and Middle Sized Enterprises in Guangdong, Guangxi, Guizhou to contribute to the construction of Foshan City as a model city for the development of the social credit system. The local government explores the construction of the personal credit system, striving to become a pilot demonstration zone of individual social credit system construction in Guangdong Province. They have constructed the credit chain of incentive and constraint mechanisms to guide the optimization and upgrading of social credit environment with institutional innovation.

Five supporting mechanisms were proposed in Nanhai District. They have built the mechanism of incentive for credit and restraints for discredit and established the listing system to make those who keep promises and those who break promises known to the public and correspondingly put forward a number of measures to encourage and constrain. Those who are on the list of credit can enjoy some priorities and preferences in the following aspects such as collecting points for their children to become temporary students, applying for public rental housing, applying for special supporting funds and government subsidies and obtaining tickets in the tourist attractions. While those on the list of discredit are denied in such aspects as high consumption, credit financing, applying for government supporting funds and participating in bidding and government procurement. In addition, the Nanhai District has launched the honesty and self-discipline mechanism, credit repair mechanism, objection handling mechanism, and so on.[3]

4. A credit services market has been standardized and cultivated

We have established a multi-level credit services organization system in which public credit services agencies and social credit services agencies complement each other and the credit information basic services complement the value-added services. We have promoted the development and innovation of the credit services products as well as their extensive applications, promoted normative development of credit registry and credit rating agencies, improved the quality of credit services and enhanced the international competitiveness of credit services. The supervision system of credit registry and credit service market has been improved. The Inner Mongolia Autonomous Region has done very well in the cultivation and standardization of credit service market. Inner Mongolia public credit services center is above the average in the credit service industry in Inner Mongolia.

Founded in March 2011, the Inner Mongolia Public Credit Services Center (hereinafter referred to as the "Center") is a powerful assistant of the government to guide and promote the construction of social credit system, the third party of credit risk identification and credit evaluation. In 2016, the Center was rated as a 5A social organization by the Inner Mongolia Autonomous Region Civil Affairs Department.

The Center's service sectors include "Credit Registry and Credit Filing", "Publicity and Education", "Investigation and Planning", "Credit Evaluation", "Overall Planning", "Credit Research", "Effect Review", "Credit Investigation", "Evaluation of Credit, Risk, Commercial Morality and Legal Person Governance", "Evaluation of Honoring the Contract and Keeping the Promise", "Inquiry on the Credit Status of Citizens and Legal Persons", "Food Safety Tracing", "Application of Credit Achievements", "Credit Code

---

3   With Credit, All the Roads Unblocked; Without Credit, All the Roads Blocked—A Documentary of the Construction of Credit System in Nanhai District, Foshan City by Liu Taishan, *People's Daily*, June 12, 2017, p. 13

Recognition", "Credit Management Training", "Credit Demonstration", "Brand Certification of Credibility" and so on.

So far, the Center has successfully developed their own credit system including credit registry system credit evaluation system, dishonesty disciplinary system, credit inquiry system, credit data exchange system, news releasing system, credit review system, credit recovery system and food safety tracing system. The Center has also compiled a professional yearbook The Inner Mongolia Credit Annals, which reflects the construction process of the credit system in Inner Mongolia Autonomous Region, studied and published Inner Mongolia Public Credit Service Models. Now the Center regularly publishes a magazine concerning credit in Inner Mongolia Autonomous Region. All these efforts have deepened the research of credit culture of Inner Mongolia Autonomous Region, filled the gap of deep study in credit research, and provided important references for our party committees, governments and enterprises to make scientific decisions.[4]

---

4 Inner Mongolia Public Credit Service Center, *Chinese Social Organizations*, 2017(4).

III. Establishing and improving the public safety system

Feeling safe in the society life is very important for both an individual and a family. Likewise, it is of great importance for both the society and the state. Strengthening the construction of peaceful China is an internal need of the society building and social governance in China. The construction of peaceful China is not only a practical need for maintaining the vital interests of people, but also an internal requirement for realizing the great rejuvenation of the Chinese nation. Xi Jinping pointed out: "After the problem of food and clothing has been solved, living in peace and safety is the primary demand of the people in the society, the most important people's wellbeing and the most fundamental environment for development."[5] In May 2013, Xi Jinping made an important instruction on the construction of a peaceful China: "We should thoroughly implement the spirit of the 18th Party Congress, place the construction of peaceful China in the overall development of the cause of socialism with Chinese characteristics to plan, closely focus on the 'two centennial' goals, take people's demand for the construction of peaceful China as the direction of our efforts, adhere to governance at source, systematic governance, comprehensive governance and law-based governance, strive to solve deep-rooted problems, focus on building a peaceful China, so as to ensure that the people live and work in peace and contentment, the society is stable and in order and the country is in enduring peace and stability."[6]

Human lives are vital and safety is paramount. Establishing and improving a sound public safety system is the main content of building a peaceful China. In order to improve the public security system, we should adhere to "putting people at the center", firmly establish the concept of safety development, raise the level of ideological awareness of the importance of public safety, take effective measures and carry out effective action to ensure the safety of the life and property of the overwhelming majority of the people. Therefore, to firmly establish the concept of safety development, we shall adhere to people's interests first. Xi Jinping pointed out: "Public safety is present everywhere. To maintain public safety, we must start by establishing

---

5 *A Series of Important Speeches by General Secretary Xi Jinping* (2016 ed.), compiled by the Publicity Department of the CPC Central Committee, People's Press, 2016, p. 223.

6 The Party Literature Research Office of the CPC Central Committee, *Excepts from Xi Jinping's Remarks on Comprehensively Deepening the Reform* (2016 ed.), Central Party Literature Press, 2014, p. 93.

and improving a long-term effective mechanism, advance the innovation in ideas and concepts, methods and means, systems and mechanisms and accelerate the improvement of the public safety system".[7] "Public safety is an important embodiment of social stability and good social order, and an important guarantee for people to live and work in peace and contentment."[8] "We should firmly establish the concept of safety development and improve the public safety system and make great efforts to reduce the threat of the public safety incidents to people's life and health."[9] On the afternoon of May 29, 2015, the Political Bureau of the CPC Central Committee organized the 23rd group study session on improving the public security system. While presiding over the learning, Xi Jinping emphasized that "Public security is linked with every household. Ensuring public security is vital to the safety of the masses' life and property and to the overall situation of stability for reform and development. We should firmly set up the concept of safety development, consciously regard the maintenance of public security as the maintenance of the fundamental interests of the public, practically do the public security work, put endeavor to build an all-dimensional and solid network of public security for the people's prosperous and contented life, a stable and well-ordered society and a state of prolonged political stability." In the *13th Five-Year Plan for Economic and Social Development of the People's Republic of China*, it is stated that "the concept of safety development should be firmly established, people's interests should be placed on the top priority, the awareness of the people's public security should be strengthened, the public safety system should be improved so as to build an all-dimensional and solid network of public security for the people's prosperous and contended life, a stable and well-ordered society and a state of prolonged political stability with an aim to build Peaceful China."

In his report to the 19th National Congress, Xi Jinping pointed out: "We should set up the idea of developing safely, promote the philosophy that life is the top priority and safety is the top concern, perfect the public security system, try every means to curb the occurrence of serious accidents and improve the ability to prevent and reduce disasters and the ability to provide disaster relief. Therefore, the Chinese government has strengthened the

---

7 Firmly Set Up and Implement the Concept of Safe Development and Safeguard People's Life and Property In All Respects, *People's Daily*, May 31, 2015, p. 1.
8 Ibid.
9 Put People's Health In the Priority of Development Strategy and Strive to Safeguard People's Health in All Respects, *People's Daily*, August 21, 2016, p. 1.

education of people's security awareness and improved the public security system and set up an all-dimensional network of public security for people's prosperous and contended life, the stable and well-ordered society, and the enduring political stability of the state to promote the construction of the Peaceful China. The Chinese government has comprehensively improved the level of safe production, dramatically improved the capacity of disaster prevention, reducing and relief, innovated the system of crime prevention and control for public security and highlighted the construction of the contingency system for emergency incidents.

1. The level of workplace safety has been raised in all respects

In order to raise the level of workplace safety in all respects, the Chinese government has established a comprehensive governance system for workplace safety featuring complete coverage in terms of responsibility, all-encompassing management, and oversight over the entire production process, and has created a permanent workplace safety mechanism. Xi Jinping pointed out: "We should be fully aware that workplace safety is an arduous, complex and pressing issue, and we must adhere to the principle of putting people and their lives first. The workplace safety responsibility system should be fully enforced, as should measures on safety management, supervision, inspection, and nsk prevention, along with incentives and punishments. We muse ensure that all Party committees and governments perform their leadership duties responsibly, that relevant government deparrments conduct proper oversight, and that enterprises assume the primary resposibility for workplace safety. As regards major risk-prone sites and industries, we should carry out targeted initiatives to strengthen safety."[10] "Party committees, governments and leading officials at all levels should be keenly aware of the importance of safety issues, and always put people's lives first. All regions, government departments, and enterprises should be relentless in applying the highest standards of workplace safety, stringently supervise workplace safety when pursuing investment and implementing projects, increase the weighting of workplace safety in performance indicators, and follow the approach of "one vote against meaning veto"[11] for ensuring work-

---

10   Firmly Set Up and Implement the Concept of Safe Development and Safeguard People's Life and Property In All Respects, *People's Daily*, May 31, 2015, p. 1.
11   A decision cannot be passed at a meeting if one attendee casts a vote against no matter how many votes are in favor. – Ed.

place safety and guarding against the risk of major work-related accidents. The responsibility of ensuring workplace safety is paramount. To reinforce the workplace safety responsibility system, senior Party and government officials should be personally involved. We must make sure that responsibility for workplace safety is assigned to relevant government departments and officials. Officials in charge of industrial sectors and officials responsible for businesses must ensure workplace safety. We should strengthen supervision and inspection concerning workplace safety, strictly implement the assessment, reward and punishment system, and constantly promote workplace safety."[12] In accordance with the spirit of these important instructions, the Chinese government has improved and implemented responsibility and assessment mechanisms as well as management systems for workplace safety, ensuring that both Party committees and governments assume responsibility, officials perform their duties while also taking responsibility for workplace safety, and those who fail to uphold safety standards are held accountable, and has ensured enterprises assume responsibility for workplace safety.

In order to raise the level of workplace safety in all respects, the Chinese government has promoted the rule of law concerning workplace safety, taken various effective measures, and comprehensively strengthened the workplace safety governance. On November 14, 2013, when inspecting the relief efforts for the Huanghuai oil pipeline accident in the Huangdao Economic Development Zone, Xi Jinping emphasized: We must maintain constant vigilance against workplace accidents, pay close attention to this problem, and guarantee without fail workplace safety, otherwise accidents will cause irreversible damage to the country and the people. We must establish a sound workplace safety responsibility system, highlight the key responsibilities of enterprises, enhance workplace safety inspections, apply lessons learned to analogous situations, and strengthen workplace safety." In recent years, the Chinese government has worked more quickly to formulate and revise workplace safety laws, regulations, and standards. It has reformed the safety evaluation system, improved multi-party mechanisms for risk control, safety hazard identification and correction, and early warning and emergency response, stepped up regulation and law enforcement efforts over workplace safety and occupational health, and worked to curb the frequent occurrence of major and

---

12 Seriously Learn from the Lessons and Focus on Learning From the Past to Comprehensively Strengthen the Work of Workplace Safety, *People's Daily*, November 25, 2013, p. 1.

serious workplace accidents. It has strengthened the systems for identifying, preventing, and dealing with safety hazards, promoted the use of information technology in workplace safety regulation, increased emergency rescue capabilities, and build capacity in respect to workplace safety inspection and oversight. It has implemented initiatives to relocate hazardous chemical plants and warehouses to ensure safe and eco-friendly production and storage of chemicals. It has strengthened basic capabilities for workplace safety such as networks for preventing and managing traffic accidents and stepped up efforts to monitor and protect the safety of important infrastructure such as telecommunications, power grids, roads, bridges, water supply facilities, and pipelines for oil and gas transmission. It has implemented an enlightenment project for raising the safety awareness of the whole society. By taking the measures mentioned above, the Chinese government has effectively curbed the occurrence of major and serious accidents in the workplace, and the mortality rate for fatal workplace accidents per unit of GDP dropped significantly.

2. The capacity for disaster prevention, mitigation and relief have been significantly improved

Disaster prevention is always given priority, and the combination of disaster prevention, fighting to mitigate the effects of disasters and providing effective relief measures is resolutely carried out. In recent years, the government has improved the comprehensive capacity of resisting natural disasters, such as meteorological disasters, flood and draught, earthquake, geological and marine disasters. It has improved the mechanism of preventing, mitigating, and providing relief for disasters, and perfected the mechanism of disaster investigating and evaluating, monitoring and early-warning, and that of preventing and dealing with emergency. Urban shelter spaces for disasters were established. The system for storing the materials for disaster relief has been improved and the level of overall utilization of resources was optimized. The establishment of the insurance system for possible catastrophes were sped up. We have developed policies concerning the social compensatory service of contingency relief, the compensation for the confiscation of materials and equipment, life insurance and pension for the casualty of the relief personnel. The publicity, education and drill for preventing and mitigating disasters were widely carried out. By enhancing these measures, the Chinese government has greatly improved its capacity for disaster prevention, mitigation and relief, and made great achievements in this field. In May 2016, *People's Daily* correspondent Pan Yue made a very good summary of these great achievements in disaster prevention, mitigation and relief in recent years.

During the 12ᵗʰ Five-Year Plan, all kinds of natural disasters occurred frequently in China. An average of 0.31 billion people came to be the victims of the disasters annually. More than 15 million people died or missed. More than 9 million people were transferred and settled down for emergency. Almost 700,000 houses collapsed. The damaged areas of crops amounted to more than 27 million hectares. The direct economic losses were over 380 billion RMB. Faced with such unpredictable conditions, an improved mechanism of preventing and mitigating disasters can build up a strong "fortress" for the safety of the masses' life and property.

Continuous improvement of the legal system for disaster mitigation and relief

"Safeguarding and improving people's wellbeing" is a meticulous and comprehensive project rather than a simple slogan, which requires constant "care" for people as a guarantee and determination and devotion to accomplish such a hard task.

Since 2014, the systems for mitigating the negative effect and providing disaster relief were constantly improved. The government (State Council) has modified the National Emergency Plan for Providing Relief in Natural Disasters. The Ministry of Civil Affairs has formulated the regulations for the working group on providing relief and emergency and modified and improved the working regulations for providing relief and contingency, relief and help in winter and spring for many times. The Ministry of Civil Affairs and the Ministry of Finance have formulated the Interim Regulations on Managing the Fund for Life Relief and Help the Victims of Natural Disasters and the Central Government's Regulations on Managing the Reserve of the Disaster Relief Materials. They have also formulated and modified numerous regulations on managing the storehouse of the disaster relief materials of the central government, on the demonstration communities of disaster reducing and on the special vehicles of the civil affairs departments for disaster emergency situations and disaster relief. Most provinces of China have formulated and issued the regulations on managing the fund for disaster relief. The mechanism for the central government and the local governments at all levels to share the fund for disaster relief proportionately has been set up. Twenty-four provinces, autonomous regions and municipalities have formulated and issued the standards for providing relief for local victims of natural disasters or implemented the experimental work.

These measures have provided a strict institutional guarantee for preventing and mitigating disasters.

Disaster prevention and mitigation is inseparable from the participation of the masses

During the five years, the National Committee for Mitigating Disasters and the Ministry of Civil Affairs have initiated the national contingency response for providing various natural disasters, adding up to 158 times. The central fund disbursed for providing relief for the victims of natural disasters added up to 49.521 billion RMB. The central government has allocated 508,000 tents, 2,422,000 quilts (beds), and 212,000 foldable beds, which has provided the solid fund and material guarantee for the emergent disaster relief, the transitional settlement, the restoration of collapsed houses and winter and spring relief.

Preliminary establishment of a rapid disaster assessment mechanism

Monitoring and early warning are important parts of contingency management for emergency. They are important foundations for improving the capacity of preventing and mitigating disasters, preventing and mitigating damages of disasters as well. With the increasing emphasis of our country on the contingency management of disasters, it is of great importance to complete the work of monitoring and predication, forecast and early warning of disasters.

A perfect system of prevention and early warning is vital to preventing and mitigating disasters. An excellent system of early warning is helpful to mitigate the destruction of disasters and to make people alert so as to prevent disasters and protect themselves better.

A series of significant decision, a great number of financial projects, and a set of warm data have shown the concern of the Party and the government to the people afflicted by natural disasters and the noble feelings of the people working in the civil affairs departments – to devote to the affairs of the public.[13]

13　Pan Yue, Improve the Disaster Prevention, Mitigation and Response Capabilities—Written Ahead of the 8th 'National Disaster Prevention and Mitigation Day', *People's Daily*, May 12, 2016, p. 11.

3. The prevention and control system for social security has been innovated in a focused manner

The innovation of the prevention and control system for social security has improved the institutional mechanisms for comprehensive social security governance. The institutions and mechanisms for the comprehensive maintenance of law and order have been improved, the establishment of a multidimensional IT-based system for crime prevention and control has been accelerated, and platforms for integrated, community-level management and services has put in place. Xi Jinping pointed out: "We should earnestly grasp the comprehensive governance of social security, adhere to the overall idea of systematic governance, law-based governance, comprehensive governance, and governance at the source, grasp cracking down on and resolving specific cases with the one hand and doing at source and basic work with the other. We should innovate the prevention and control system for social security, optimize the social environment for the public security governance, and strive to solve the deep-seated problems affecting social security."[14] Efforts to apply information technology in community-level police work have been stepped up, concrete results in the field have been achieved, procedure-based law enforcement has been ensured, and the professional organization of the police force has been strengthened. Crime prevention and control networks based on public efforts as well as cooperation between the public and police has been built up, the development of online systems for comprehensive crime prevention and control has been accelerated, and the construction of a comprehensive online prevention and control system has been accelerated and advanced. Joint law and order efforts and problem identification and resolution in key locations, sectors, and regions have been initiated. Basic capabilities for cracking down on crime, fighting against drugs, and preventing and handling cults have been strengthened. In strengthening the construction of the prevention and control system for social security and ensuring public security and social stability in an innovative way, the practice of Beijing, the capital of China, can be said to be matchless.

---

14   Firmly Set Up and Implement the Concept of Safe Development and Safeguard the Safety of People's Life and Property, *People's Daily*, May 31, 2015, p. 1.

In 2015, "Xicheng Aunties" had provided thousands of clues for the police and assisted the police officers in arresting 1,425 suspects. The picture shows that a policeman and "Xicheng Aunties" are patrolling in the neighborhood of Xijiaomin Lane.

The capital of China is known as one of the safest cities in the world. For a mega city with a population of more than 20 million, sustainable security and stability begin with the all-round management of "risk factors".

The government leads, the public participates and the whole society collaborates, with big events pulling, high technology leading and grid-based building. From security to peace, the capital's security management has been transformed from simple public security precautions to comprehensive social governance.

"Xicheng Aunties": The most important job is to "spot anything abnormal"

A million of safety volunteers, the elders who wear red hats, constitute the grounding of the capital's security. Xicheng, with an area of 50 square kilometers, is located in the central part of Beijing. There are more than 50,000 registered security volunteers in this district. Their age ranges from 58 to 65 years. Among them, females amount to more than 70 percent. "Xicheng Aunties" are named after that. What do the aunts with red hats do? They are in charge of daily inspection of communities and maintaining order on holidays. They are information assistants of security and stability, mediators of disputes, inspectors of the city's operation, publicity agents of policies and laws, and assistants who serve the communities. Among this group of "Small Red Hats" are retired women, those who are in charge of parking lots in the streets and lanes, traffic police assistants, cleaners, maintenance workers and storekeepers. In the first six months of 2015, "Small Red Hats" have collected 11,937 pieces of information and 567 clues of illegal activities. A million of "Small Red Hats" are building together a "Safe Great Wall" in the streets of Beijing.

"SWAT": 24-hour presence on the streets, response time "deployed within seconds"

"We fight against crimes and serve the public. The tourists have special confidence in us," said Gu Shuying proudly, the captain of the first mobile team of the SWAT Corps of Beijing Municipal Public Security Bureau. There are three of them in a squad. They are stationed on the streets 24 hours a day, mainly responsible for the reinforcement tasks of tackling difficulties, catching and "One-minute Handling" in the Wangfujing area. "Quick response, Quick reach, Quick screening and Quick handling", the "4Q" SWATs are armed with live ammunition, and "shooting within three seconds" is their basic skill.

Just at the same intersection, opposite to the SWATs, there is a white car for dealing with emergency situation, with two red words "Armed Police". It turns out that Beijing Municipal Public Security Bureau has set up a mechanism for the police officers and armed police officers to be on duty together according to the requirement of "disposing emergency within one minute". In fourteen important spots of Beijing such as Wang Fujing Anenue and Xidan shopping center, armed police officers are assigned to safeguard public order. The police officers, who are stationed in these spots are composed of both civil police and armed police. They implement patrol accompanied of police dogs and are well equipped.

With their ranks eliminated and management reformed, SWAT special security forces can now react to a threat within several seconds. Beijing Municipal Public Security Bureau has exercised a point-to-point and visible vertical command. The standards for work and operating processes are regulated one by one. All professional forces, including anti-terrorism, criminal investigation, EOD, obstacles clearance, firefighting and rescuing, and vehicles are arranged ready 24 hours ahead. All armed vehicles and policemen of nearby police stations are incorporated into the command structure. Dependent upon GPS, all the vehicles and police officers on duty in the streets can be coordinated and deployed from the neighborhood to the nearest location where they are needed.

"Our goal is to make distance and time measurement as accurate as possible, making them accurate enough to meter and second. We will utilize various means, hold the zero-tolerance attitude, and carry out measures firmly and resolutely to dispose the emergency of terrorism or violence to the maximum of efforts and within the minimum of duration, to ensure the safety of the masses' life and property," said Cao Zhigang, the deputy commander of the Anti-Terrorism Corps of Beijing Municipal Public Security Bureau.

It is acknowledged that Beijing Police carries out a closed rotation training for the police officers who hold the posts of "One-minute Handling", in which they are registered with real names. In the anti-riot gun training, only those who can hit the target with all five bullets within 90 seconds can pass.

"Chaoyang Masses": "Eyes" are present everywhere

More famous than the "Xicheng Aunties" are the "Chaoyang Masses". In recent years, they have reported numerous cases to the police, including the thefts and defrauding on the roadside and the celebrities' drug abuse about which the public are concerned.

The core of "Chaoyang Masses" is composed of the volunteers of social security coming from districts to small towns, from streets to villages and communities, which is 3 percent of the permanent residing population. In addition to the prizes based on comparing and assessing the mass prevention and mass treatment implemented in the city, Chaoyang District has set up a fund of 3 million RMB for awarding the public security volunteers.

At present, in many communities of the Chaoyang District, when new residents move in, warm-hearted neighbors will take the initiative to greet them, ask about their situation and offer assistance. To the ordinary people, the kindness and warmth make them feel that "a distant relative is no better than a close neighbor". To the outlaws, they are faced with the "sharp eyes of the masses". Even the slightest careless word and deed may expose themselves. This is the secret of the "Chaoyang Masses".

Command hall of the Traffic Administration Bureau: Ensure traffic security and make efforts in the sky and on the ground at the same time

In the command hall of the Traffic Administration Bureau of Beijing Municipal Public Security Bureau located in the second West Ring, on a three-story-high large screen, the situation of the road network of the whole Beijing and the real-time position of the road traffic police are clearly displayed. The Command and Dispatch Section staff on duty is looking at the monitor, constantly switching between the images of the roadside cameras.

Han Lei, a staff of the Command and Dispatch Section, introduced that the command hall of the Traffic Administration Bureau can mobilize any traffic police officer on duty in the area under the jurisdiction of Beijing by means of the intelligent commanding system. In turn, all traffic police officers on duty can report information to their subordinate units and superior departments in real time through their own telephone. In case of major emergencies, all kinds of police or any single officer of the Beijing Municipal Public Security Bureau can directly report to the Bureau through the "One Report, Direct Report" mechanism. The Duty Command Center of the Bureau shall give unified command to all kinds of police in real time according to the situation.

The "Pharaohs": Resolve contradictions early at the grassroots

Before retiring, 79-year-old Yang Tingchun was the president of the Beijing First Intermediate People's Court. Today, he is among the twelve retired judges who hold free legal advice sessions on the third Thursday of every month on the ground floor of Building 24 in the Jiaheyuan district. The oldest of them is 83 years old and the youngest is 58 years old, and they are respected by the public as the "Pharaohs".

"With economic and social development, it is inevitable that conflicts will increase. The key is to resolve them in accordance with the law and at an early stage." Some of the retired and laid-off workers who sought help were unable to consult a lawyer because of their lack of legal knowledge and weak financial means. They often turned small conflicts into big ones, and their interests are not protected, which made Yang Tingchun very worried. Xiao Zhang, who left his hometown to work in Beijing, once counseled for his unpaid wages and said, "he will resort to violence, if there is no solution". The judges patiently explained him that "the gains of violence are not worth the losses" and persuaded him. Later, Xiao Zhang got his salary through arbitration according to the guidelines and specially called President Yang to report that he "trusts the law".

For more than 10 years, the "Pharaohs" have served more than 10 thousand people. Even people from other provinces and cities have come to consult them. With the increase of the residents who know, understand and trust the law, Pannan community already became a civilized community in the city and an advanced community for comprehensive governance.

Nowadays, the methods and mechanism, such as the "Pharaohs", the "Citizen Advising Team" and the "Community Roundtable" have become a number of methods and mechanisms to resolve conflicts at the grassroots and nip them in the bud, becoming a miniature "pressure reducer" for community peace and urban peace.

Shuangyushu Fire Brigade: Rescue in case of any disaster, help in case of any trouble – the alarm is the horn

It was just before dawn late in the midnight. However, Dai Yaqiang, a firefighter for fifteen years, without any trace of sleepiness, is ready to show up at any time. He had long been used to living according to the police situation. "No matter what time, as long as the bell rings, the situation will come."

Shuangyushu Fire Brigade is responsible for the safety of a district with 36 square kilometers and fifty-five officers and firemen. This Brigade dealt with 1,587 cases in 2014. "Whenever we reached the fire site, we knew nothing about what risks we would be faced with. Emergence or urgency status is our normalcy and we are not allowed to think about the dangers." Dai Yaqiang said: "In many cases, to live or to die is merely decided in a few seconds."

Jin Yulei, a vice-leader of the Brigade, has worked in the brigade for many years. He is experienced and knowledgeable. However, when he opened a door on the scene of fire not long ago, a flashover suddenly occurred and his respirator was knocked out. Fortunately, he made a narrow escape. Ten days later, he married his bride.

Fire brigades exercise fire services administration, rush to deal with fire emergency, handle emergency and fight against terrorists, and serve the public. There are more than seven thousand officers and soldiers in the Fireman Corps of Beijing Police. The thirty-eight basic skills have made muscular men out of the firemen. Fifty-two practical operation of working teams and groups have made them cooperate well enough to handle various emergency on spot. The eight kinds of professional teams for providing relief in the air, in the waters, in the mountains, and in the subway, and the assaulting and storm troop composed of eight hundred members can provide relief in all areas. Telephone services of 119, 110, 122 and 120 are interlinked and the teams can act together for emergency in a coordinated mechanism. Apart from this, the mechanism of cross-district police cooperation and the mechanism of 24-hour duty for major safety situations ensure swift reaction and can mobilize full equipped rescue and relief forces in to the fifty-two key areas of the city.

The firemen risk their lives in providing relief and serve the public within every possible way. "Besides fighting against fire, we also receive reports of other emergencies that need our rescue and relief. On the 17th, we rushed to the scene four times, of which we helped the public deal with their difficulties twice." According to Dai Yaqiang's introduction, there are more than 2,000 tools on the demolition truck they are equipped with, "there is everything ranging from the ring-cutting device invented by the firemen themselves to the huge cranes".

Beixinqiao Police Station and the On-Duty Office of Network Security: From the reality to the virtual world – it's an exception not to work overtime

24 hours a day is the norm for all grassroots police stations in Beijing, and Gui Street is particularly busy in the early hours of the morning. As police officers at the Beixinqiao Police Station in Beijing's Dongcheng District, Zhou Lei and Xue Junbo's jurisdiction includes 12 communities and Gui Street, a night catering street with more than 300 restaurants. In 18 hours, Zhou Lei and Xue Junbo's 10 person shift team has handled more than 40 police cases of all kinds.

Like Zhou Lei and Xue Junbo, Wu Yue, an Internet policeman of the Network Security Team of the Beijing Municipal Public Security Bureau is also on duty. But unlike the police officers in the police station, as the administrator Weibo and Weibo accounts of the "Beijing Internet Police", for Wu Yue, the computer is the front line and the Internet is the battlefield.

Beijing is home to more than 70% of the country's large portals, with state ministries and commissions gathering and corporate headquarters, which means greater responsibility for the capital's Internet police. Whenever there are sudden and sensitive major cases and events, the Beijing Internet Security Headquarters will immediately carry out search and disinformation work against all kinds of false information. For example, in the recent past, Wu Yue and his colleagues have been very busy in their work and dare not relax for a moment. According to statistics, since August, the "Beijing Internet Police" has had 28,370 exchanges and interactions, 12,307 reports have been received, 148 netizens have been warned, and 2,280 illegal information has been involved.

Fengheying Checkpoint into the capital: Closely manage all entries into Beijing

The day just breaks and the sun rises slowly from the east. A huge blue dome covers the spot of 45.3 kilometer of No. 104 national highway. Zheng Jie in neat uniform sits by the intersection, is taking pictures with a machine of the chassis of the vehicles that are entering the capital. It only takes one second to complete the checking on the vehicles. The details on the chassis can be investigated by enlarging the pictures on the screen.

Fengheying Public Security Checkpoint is the southeastern gate of Beijing. Every day 15,000 vehicles on average go through the station to enter the capital. Zheng Jie is an instructor of the inspection station.

It is known that since May 2015, Beijing Municipal Public Security Bureau, taking the lead in relevant departments, has newly built 23 public security checkpoints in addition to renovating the former 22 peripheral checkpoints for entering the capital and stationing 11 comprehensive checkpoints. Fengheying Public Security Checkpoint is one of the newly built checkpoints.

Since the end of July 2015, the construction of the peripheral defense line for checking and controlling public security has been initiated in Beijing, investigating 196 roads leading to Beijing. All the roads came to be administrated closely, in which points were set up and responsibility was specified to persons. All the roads entering the capital are covered, checked and controlled around the clock, which is a normal practice. Seventy-eight suspects have been arrested for breaking laws and committing crimes.

The sunlight is shining on the earth and a new day to guard the security of the capital starts.[15]

---

15   Who is Guarding the Safety of the Capital (People's Eye· Focus of this Issue· Safety Construction by Zhu Jingruo, Wang Haonan and Yu Ronghua), *People's Daily*, August, 21, 2015, p. 16.

Innovation never ends. Xi Jinping emphasized: "Innovation is the soul of a nation's progress, the inexhaustible force enhancing a country's prosperity, and indeed the profound endowment of the Chinese nation".[16] The innovation of the system of preventing and controlling social security never stops, either. In terms of the "Chaoyang Masses" alone, the launch of the Chaoyang Masses APP became an innovative highlight in the construction of the prevention and control system for social security in the first half of 2017.

The news of Chaoyang residents receiving APPs on-line caused a heated discussion on the network. The index of searching on blogs increased dramatically on the second day of its appearance on the line. Relevant topics have been read more than two million times. Netizens made a lot of comments, "Terrific! My 'Chaoyang Masses'".

The "Chaoyang Masses" APP is developed by the Police of Chaoyang District of Beijing and relevant units. It is an integrated platform for the police and the public to cooperate, to issue cases, and for the public to upload. The police officers together with the public collect clues of cases and receive the reports on anything suspicious. Thus, the police can provide a comprehensive information-sharing service for social security, urban development, and the safety of the masses' life and property.

Let the masses become "mobile cameras"

Over the past few years, the "Chaoyang Masses" have been frequently mentioned in the bulletin of crimes by the police for their reports on clues of illegal activities. They have literally become the instant "online celebrities".

When you open the "Chaoyang Masses" APP, you can see the words "everything is dependent on the public and for the public and everything is for serving the public". There are five columns on its home page, which are Major Cases, Missing Person, Lost and Found, Suspects, Vehicles. On the lower right corner of the home page, there is a marked icon of "Tip Off". Click the icon, you can see the classification of "Child Trafficking", "Possible Suspects", "Elderly Missing Person", "Traffic Violations", "Lost and Found", "Other Tip-offs", etc. After registration, the user can report with characters, pictures, videos.

"The launch of the 'Chaoyang Masses' APP represents a philosophy that the policing work at the grassroots level should mobilize the masses and rely

---

16 Xi Jinping, *The Governance of China*, Foreign Languages Press, 2014, p. 59.

On February 13, 2017, The Chaoyang Branch of Beijing Municipal Public Security Bureau issued a message through the microblog "Safe Chaoyang". In order to further close the relationship between the police and the public and better play the role of "Chaoyang Masses", the Chaoyang Police and relevant units have developed the "Chaoyang Masses HD" APP .

on the masses. It closely links the government's public security management with the daily life of the masses. It can arouse the masses' enthusiasm for participation in governance and lets the government and society achieve an effective benign interaction", commented Huang Heng, an associate professor of School of Government at Peking University.[17]

4. The construction of a system of emergency response to sudden incidents has been strengthened

In order to perfect the public security system, the Chinese government has set up a contingency system for emergency that matches with the risk of public security, covers the entire process of emergency management and involves the participation of the whole society. In order to promote the construction of the contingency system for emergency, the government has

17   Dong Siyu, "Chaoyang Masses" APP Becomes an Online Hit, *People's Daily*, March 16, 2017, p. 14.

strengthened the construction of the basic capabilities of contingency, set up and improved the risk management and control system of major sources of dangers and important infrastructure facilities. Thus, the ability to release early warning for emergency and to complete the contingency reaction has been enhanced and the level of the grassroots contingency management has been greatly raised. The construction of the capability to meet emergency of terrorism in large and medium-sized cities has been strengthened, too. The competency of dealing with emergency such as hazardous chemicals, oil spilled over the sea, searching and salvaging in the waters, contingency for nuclear accidents, emergent medical relief has been highlighted and the capability of coordinating and guaranteeing contingency resources has been enhanced, too. The system of compensating the contingency collection and confiscation has been set up. The management of contingency volunteers has been improved and the project of improving the public's capability of self-relief and mutual relief has been carried out. The competency of handling emergency abroad involving our country has been improved. The construction of the contingency system for emergency and the timely and accurate release of early warning information are important links to handle emergency effectively. The establishment and operation of the National Center for Early Warning Information Release has set a model that can be drawn for releasing information timely and accurately to handle emergency.

In May 2015, the National Center for Early Warning Information Release was put into operation. Being an emergency management agency of the State Council, the center is an authorized releasing agency of providing comprehensive early warning for the personnel who are in charge of emergency in the governmental agency and the public as well.

Authoritative release: Make emergency monitoring and early warning more standardized

In early July 2015, Typhoon Lotus and Typhoon Canhong landed on the southeastern coast of China successively, which became a huge test for the newly built National Center for Early Warning Information Release.

Han Xiao, a staff of the Office of Operating and Controlling of Early Warning Information Release Center told the reporter that during the period affected by Typhoon Lotus and Typhoon Canhong, the national system of releasing early warning information for emergency amounted to 1,010 pieces.

Among the information, there were 17 pieces of early warning information released at national level and 993 pieces issued by the provinces. The National Center for Early Warning Information Release successfully passed the test successfully and performed its function.

The establishment of the Early Warning Information Release Center symbolized that the early warning information release of emergency of China has stepped into a normalized stage.

Timely release: Early warning information can reach the public within 1 minute

The early warning information is produced by the relevant departments of the State Council, such as that of diplomacy, health and family planning, earthquake, or marine, according to the emergency plan or the provisions concerning specific business of these departments. They set up the cooperative mechanism with the Early Warning Information Release Center and release early warning information to the public through the national system of releasing early warning for emergency.

Improve the network: Standardize each link of early warning-production, release and transmission

The release of early warning information is linked up from top to bottom. In the system, it can be shared from the county level to the city, province and national level, and also be sent from the national level to the province, city and county level, and realizes the up-and-down sharing of warning information.

"The release of early warning information is an important component of the contingency work. It is a common responsibility of the government and the society rather than a job exclusive to some agency." Sun Jian, the dean of the National Center for Early Warning Information Release stated that all departments and local governments should attach importance to it. They should strengthen their efforts in the institution-building, personnel and policy support, etc. They should ensure that early warning information can be timely transmitted to the people easily stricken by disasters and those disadvantaged groups so as to deal with the problem of "the last kilometer" for the release of early warning information.[18]

---

18 Kou Jiangze, The Platform to Give Crisis-Warning Came into Being (Green Focus–Meteorological Disaster Prevention and Mitigation, *People's Daily*, August 8, 2015, p. 10.

IV. Establishing a national security system

In his report to the 19th National Congress, Xi Jinping emphatically pointed out: "The safety of the country is the important cornerstone of keeping the country in stability. Safeguarding the national security is the fundamental interest of all the ethnic groups." National security is the foundation of building a country and an important guarantee for a country's survival and development. In addition, national security is a fundamental guarantee for a stable development of society and the safety and well-being of the people. It is an essential foundation for internal affairs and diplomacy and can bring peace and stability to a country. Xi Jinping emphasized that, "Enhancing the sense of crisis and being vigilant even in peace time is an important principle that must be held continuously for administrating the Party and the State. To consolidate its ruling status, our Party should unite the people and lead them to insist and develop the socialism with Chinese characteristics. Safeguarding national security is a matter of primary importance."[112] Therefore, the Third Plenary Session of the 18th CPC Central Committee made a strategic planning that "a National Security Commission is to be established to perfect the national security system and the national security strategies to safeguard national security".

We should enhance the sense of crisis and the sense of risk and remain vigilant in peace time and be prepared against want. We should fully put into effect the integrative national security concept, implement a national security strategy, and keep working to improve our ability to ensure national security, so as to effectively safeguard Chinese national security. Xi Jinping emphasized that, "the Third Plenary Session of the 18th CPC Central Committee decided to establish the National Security Commission, which is an urgent demand for promoting the modernization of the national administration system and the competency for administration so as to ensure the state's long-term stability and order. It is also an important guarantee for building a moderately prosperous society in all aspects and fulfilling the Chinese Dream—great national rejuvenation of the Chinese nation. It aims at adapting to the new situation and new task that the national security of our country is faced with, setting up a centralized, unified, efficient and authoritative system of national security, and strengthening the leadership of national security work."[19] In the *13th Five-Year Plan for Economic and Social Development of the People's Republic of China*, it is stated "to fully put into effect the integrative national security concept, implement a national security strategy, and keep working to improve our ability to ensure national security, so as to effectively safeguard Chinese national security." The integrative national security concept emphasizes that we should take people's security as our aim, political security as the root, economic security as the foundation, military, cultural and social security as the guarantee, promotion of international security as the support to maintain national security in all fields.

The 19th CPC National Congress pointed out: "We will improve state security strategies and policies, firmly maintain national politics security, make an overall plan to push forward all the security works, improve national security system, strengthen the rule of law guarantees of national security and improve the ability to prevent and protect against security risks." The establishment of the national security system needs to continuously improve the systems and mechanisms of safeguarding national security, actively strengthen the construction of the rule of law concerning national security, and embark on the road of national security with Chinese characteristics.

1. Systems and mechanisms for safeguarding national security have been improved

In order to perfect the systems and mechanisms for safeguarding national security, national security policies in key areas including the political, territorial, economic, social, resource-, and internet- related fields have been formulated and implemented, medium-term and long-term security objectives, policies, and measures for these areas have been defined, and the ability to respond to all kinds of risks and challenges has been strengthened. The construction of national security science, technology, and equipment has been strengthened, a sound national security monitoring and early-warning system has been established, the integration between monitoring and early-warning systems in different areas to increase efficiency has been tightened, and the security information gathering, analysis, and processing capabilities have been improved. Xi Jinping emphasized that "the present

---

19 Adhere to the Concept of Comprehensive National Security and Take the Road of National Security with Chinese Characteristics, *People's Daily*, April16, 2014, p. 1.

connotation and extension of our country's national security are richer than any time in history. Its space and time scope are the widest in history. The internal and external factors are the most sophisticated in history. We must pursue the holistic approach of national security, take the people's security as the purpose, political security as the root, economic security as the foundation, military, cultural and social security as the guarantee, promotion of international security as the support, and take the road of national security with Chinese characteristics. The practical implementation of the holistic approach of national security needs placing the emphasis on external security as well as internal security. Internally, we should pursue development, reform, stability and build Peaceful China. Externally, we should pursue peace, cooperation, win-to-win and build harmonious world. We should not only pay attention to the security of territory, but also the security of the people. We should take the people as the root, hold that national security is for the people and everything relies on the people so as to lay a solid foundation of the masses for national security. We should pay attention to traditional security as well as non-traditional security. We should set up an integrated system of national security covering political security, territorial security, military security, economic security, cultural security, social security, scientific and technological security, information security, ecological security, resource security and nuclear security. We should pay attention to the issue of security as well as the issue of development. Development is the basis of security while security is the condition of development. Making the nation rich can make the army powerful and making a powerful army can defend the nation. We should pay attention to both our own security and the common security so as to forge a community of common destiny so as to promote all parties to move together to the goals of mutual benefits and mutual security."[20]

In order to improve the system and mechanisms of safeguarding national security, the system of early warning of external risks classified and ranked has been established. The monitoring and assessment of major security risks has been highlighted and the contingency-handling plan for major risks of national security has been made. The system and mechanism of national security investigation has been perfected. The assessment of the security risks in major fields, major reforms, major projects, major programs and major

---

20 Ibid.

polices has been completed. The coordinating mechanism for maintaining national security in key fields has been set up to enhance the organization and coordination of national security work.

2. The security and sovereignty of the political power have been safeguarded

In order to safeguard the security and sovereignty of the political power, a sound trans-departmental, trans-regional joint work mechanism to resolutely prevent and take severe action in accordance with the law against infiltration, subversion, and sabotage by hostile forces, violent terrorist activities, ethnic separatist activities, and religious extremist activities has been set up. Xi Jinping emphasized: "Countering terrorism has a direct bearing on national security, the people's immediate interests, and reform, development and stability. The battle against terrorism safeguards national unity, social stability and the people's well-being. We must take decisive measures in deterring terrorism and keep up the pressure to thwart terrorism. We should work out a sound anti-terrorism work pattern, improve our anti-terrorism work system and build up our anti-terrorism strength. We should enlist both professional forces and the public in the fight against terrorism, get the general public to carry out different forms of activities against terrorism, build an impregnable anti-terrorism network, and ensure that terrorists are hunted down like rats. We should also let patriotic religious personages play a role, enhance positive guidance for religious believers, meet the latter's normal religious needs, and effectively resist the infiltration of religious extremism."[21] To this end, China has strengthened the construction of professional anti-terrorism forces, enhanced international cooperation on combating terrorism, strengthened anti-espionage work, intensified the fight against the hostile forces in the on-line sovereignty defense and the management and control of public opinions on Internet curbing the infiltration and sabotage activities carried out by hostile and terrorist forces using cyberspace. The construction of a technical defense system at the border was strengthened. We have attached great importance to doing a good job in the ideological field and effectively maintained ideological security.

In order to safeguard the security and sovereignty of the political power,

---

21　Practically Maintain National Security and Social Stability and Create Good Social Environment for Realizing the Objectives, *People's Daily*, April 27, 2014, p. 1.

terrorism is resolutely combated. The fight against terrorism is related to national security. We must deal a devastating blow to violent terrorist forces and never be soft hearted. In dealing with terrorism, we have struck hard at the sight of "fear", dealt heavy blows, resolutely suppressed the arrogance of violent terrorists, deterred the enemy and inspired the people. Meanwhile, we have strengthened international cooperation on combating terrorism and jointly built an iron wall against terrorism. As Xi Jinping emphasized: "Terrorism denies basic human rights, tramples on humanitarian justice and challenges the shared norms of human civilization. It is not an issue of ethnicity, nor an issue of religion. Terrorists are the common enemy of people of all ethnic groups. We should firmly trust and rely on the officials and the general public of all ethnic groups, and unite with them in safeguarding ethnic unity and social stability."[22] Therefore, China has resolutely suppressed and cracked down the activities of separation, infiltration, destruction and subversion undertaken by the hostile forces at home and abroad in the name of ethnic issue or religion. Thus, we have ensured the safety of the people's life and property, ensured the harmonious, stable, and healthy development of the society and safeguarded the security and sovereignty of the political power.

3. Economic security risks have been fended off and defused

In an era of economic globalization, national economic security is of great importance. National economic security belongs to the scope of national security. National economic security refers both to the state when a state's economic strength and development is under no fundamental threat, and to the state when a state that its economy maintains an independent and stable operation, can provide an effective supply of resources necessary for its economic existence and development, and its overall economic welfare is under no vicious infringement.

In order to fend off and defuse the risks of national economic security and take the guarantee of economic security as a focus, China has actively maintained the state's basic economic system and the order of socialist market economy. The system and mechanisms of fending off and defusing economic security risks have been established, which has guaranteed the

---

22 Ibid.

security of important business, key fields, key industries, major infrastructure and major construction projects, and other major economic interests that are essential to national economy. Upholding the principle that we must be aware of our bottom line and put prevention first, national economic security in areas such as strategic resources, key industries, finance and banking, and cross-border capital flow has been safeguarded. The dynamic monitoring and analysis of key economic indicators has been strengthened and an emergency plan for responding to risks in major economic sectors has been formulated. The government has coordinated responses to fiscal and financial risks that arise as we work to address overcapacity, reduce commodity housing stock, and carried out debt deleveraging, thus working proactively to diffuse risks both in a controlled manner and at a controlled pace.

In order to fend off and defuse national economic security risks, the regulation over and response to both unusual fluctuations and risk transference in the financial market and risks that come with new forms of financial business have been strengthened. The unified management of governmental debt has been perfected, the market-based transformation of local government financing platforms has been pushed forward, and the risks posed by local government debt have been effectively defused. It has been ensured that there are more options for dealing with non-performing assets in the banking sector, the tools and emergency plans for managing liquidity risks have been improved, and illegal fundraising has been cracked down. Enterprise debt risks have been fended off and defused. The ability to prevent and control risks in areas such as energy, mineral resources, water resources, grain, ecological conservation, environmental protection, workplace safety, and the internet has been improved. The country's reserves of strategic goods and create a national strategic resource and energy reserve system based on a combination of reserve goods, production capacity, and production locations has been improved.

4. The construction of rule of law concerning national security has been strengthened

National security means that a state's political power, sovereignty, unity and territorial integrity, the people's welfare, the sustainable development of economy and society, and other major interests of the country are state of being free from danger and free from internal and external threats as well as the capacity to safeguard a continuous state of security. It also refers to the ability of a nation to maintain a sustainable state of security. In order to safeguard national security, we should pursue the holistic approach to national security with the people's security as the ultimate purpose, political security as the root, economic security as the basis, military, cultural and social security as the guarantee and the promotion of international security as the backing, maintain national security in all fields, build the national security system and progress along the path of national security with Chinese characteristics.

Rule of law is the best way to administrate the country and manage state affairs. National security needs to be safeguarded by the rule of law. On July 1, 2015 the Standing Committee of the 12th National People's Congress has passed the *National Security Law of the People's Republic of China*, and issued relevant rules for its implementation. Meanwhile, the Chinese government has promoted the legislation on national economic security, non-proliferation, national intelligence, network security, export control, registration of foreign agents, inspection of foreign capital, etc., that concern national security. The legal system of national security has been perfected quickly so as to fully utilize legal means to maintain national security. As to the construction of rule of law concerning national security, Zhang Dejiang made the *Work Report of the Standing Committee of National People's Congress* on the Fifth Session of the 12th National People's Congress on March 8, 2017. In the work report, he emphasized that the construction of the legal system of national security has made important advancement. National security is the footstone for bringing peace and stability to the country. The Standing Committee has carried out the holistic approach of national security, stuck to starting from the national conditions and reality, maintained political consistency, seized the opportunity of legislation and speeded up the construction of rule of law concerning national security. In

2014 and 2015, the *Counterespionage Law of the People's Republic of China*, the *National Security Law of the People's Republic of China*, and the *Anti-terrorism Law of the People's Republic of China* were promulgated. In 2016, the *Law of the People's Republic of China on the Administration of Overseas Non-Governmental Organizations' Activities in the Territory of China*, the *Network Security Law of the People's Republic of China and the Law on National Defense Transportation of the People's Republic of China* have been deliberated and ratified. And the *National Intelligence Law of the People's Republic of China and the Law of the People's Republic of China on Nuclear Security (Draft)* have been considered.[23]

Ultimately, the work of national security should adhere to "putting people at the center" and provide solid political guarantee for the people to live and work in contentment. Adherence to "putting people at the center" shows the ultimate value orientation of national security work, that is, to continuously enhance the people's sense of security, sense of contentment and sense of happiness. We should think and act on legalization to strengthen national security. The maintenance of national security needs to strengthen the awareness of rule of law and maintain national security according to law. We should highlight the construction of the legalization of national security. As to legislation, laws and regulations relevant to national security should be made to complete a systematic, all-round, and well-operating legal system of national security. As to enforcement, the organizations and agencies of national security should carefully implement relevant laws and fulfill their legal duty and obligation to maintain national security according to law. In adhering to law, we should enhance the publicity and education of the laws and regulations relevant to national security, such as the international security law and the anti-terrorism law to enhance the people's concept of maintaining national security according to law. In addition, we should highlight the people's awareness of national security and mobilize the whole society to maintain national security together by relying on the rule of law.

---

23 Zhang Dejiang, Work Report of the Standing Committee of the National People's Congress - at the Fifth Session of the 12th National People's Congress, *People's Daily*, March 19, 2017, p. 1.

Conclusion

In his report to the 19th CPC National Congress Xi Jinping emphasized: "In our Party, each and every one of us must always breathe the same breath as the people, share the same future, and stay truly connected to them. The aspirations of the people to live a better life must always be the focus of our efforts. We must keep on striving with endless energy toward the great goal of national rejuvenation." Implementing the great spirit of the 19th CPC National Congress, the fundamental point to strengthen the society building and social governance in China lies in continuously raising and safeguarding and improving people's wellbeing, staying true to the original aspiration and benefiting the people.

Xi Jinping pointed out: "Leading the people to create a happy life is the unswerving goal of our party. We must conform to the people's yearning for a better life, adhere to the people-centered development concept, focus on safeguarding and improving people's wellbeing, develop various social undertakings, increase income distribution adjustments, win the battle against poverty, and ensure people's equality. Participate and equal rights to development, so that the results of reform and development will benefit all the people more and more equitably, and move steadily towards the goal of achieving common prosperity for all people."[1]

Founded on the basis of the society building ideas of Marx, Engels and Mao Zedong and on the basis of the theories of society building since the

---

1 Xi Jinping's Speech at the Conference for the 95th Anniversary of the Founding of the Communist Party of China (July 1, 2016), *People's Daily*, July 2, 2016, p. 2.

Reform and Opening-up, the society building and social governance in China – regardless of whether focusing on improving the level of education and health of the entire population and improving the people's wellbeing or on building a social governance system with Chinese characteristics and strengthening and innovating social governance – the starting points and footholds lie in to moving on forward without forgetting the original aspiration, adhering to "putting people at the center", promoting the sharing of the fruits of development by all, and achieving common prosperity for all people. In China, the Communist Party of China's leadership is the fundamental political guarantee for the ultimate achievement of common prosperity for all people.

The ideational source of the society building in China is the idea of relying on the "association of free men", promoting man's free and comprehensive development and ultimately achieving communism. Mao Zedong's ideas of society building have provided a rich ideological basis for the the theories of society building since China's Reform and Opening-up. At present, the the society building and social governance in China are still in the primary stage of socialism, the level of social productive forces is still low, and material wealth has not achieved a full abundance yet. Therefore, the society building and social governance in China are still on the way. Since the 18th CPC National Congress, the CPC has led the Chinese people to enter the new era of socialism with Chinese characteristics, the era of society building and social governance, continuously pushing forward the innovation and development of the society building and social governance in China and has already made brilliant achievements, which is obvious to the whole world.

From Marxism-Leninism to Mao Zedong Thought, from Deng Xiaoping Theory and the important thought of "Three Represents" to the Scientific Concept on Development, and then to the Xi Jinping's Thought on Socialism with Chinese Characteristics for a New Era which is currently implemented in China, as the guiding ideology of the Communist Party of China, running through Marxism-Leninism and the red line and core of Mao Zedong Thought and the theoretical system of socialism with Chinese characteristics it is the four words: "all for the people". The people are both the foundation of power of revolution, construction, reform and development and also the ultimate purpose for the CPC to carry out revolution, construction, reform and development. Therefore, Xi Jinping solemnly pointed out: "To stay true to our original aspiration, continue to move forward, we firmly believe that the Party is rooted in the people and its power comes from the people; adhere to the principles of all for the people and all depends on the people; give full play to the people's initiatives and creativity; and continuously advance the cause to benefit the people."[2] Adhering to "putting people at the center" and following Xi Jinping's instruction "Letting the people live a good life is the starting point and stop-over point of all our work"[3], the Communist Party of China will advance the society building and social governance in China and continue to make more brilliant great achievements.

Historical materialism holds that the people are the creators of history and the true driving force of for the history to develop forward. Therefore, Marx and Engels called on "Workers of the world, unite"! Mao Zedong led the Chinese people to carry out the Chinese revolution and construction, pushed forward society building in China to develop forward, and insisted that "People, only the people, are the driving force creating world history" and "Long live the people"! and that the Chinese Communists should serve the people whole-heartedly. From "I am a son of the Chinese People. I deeply love my motherland and people" to "advancing man's comprehensive development", from "taking human as foundation" to "putting people at the center", all of them highlight the profound feelings and pure devotion of "all for the people" of several generations of CPC leaders to the Chinese people.

"Standing on the people's side represents the fundamental political stance of the Communist Party of China, and it is what distinguishes a Marxist political party from other political parties."[4] Since the birth of the Communist Party of China, on its high-flying banner it is written "for the benefit of the people", and it has adhered to "putting the people at the center" in the practice of revolution, construction, reform, and development. It is the Chinese people who are pushing forward the great practice of the society building and social governance in China and creating great Chinese history. In China, the

---

2 Xi Jinping's Speech at the Conference for the 95th Anniversary of the Founding of the Communist Party of China (July 1, 2016), *People's Daily*, July 2, 2016, p. 2.

3 Implement the Innovation-Driven Development Strategy and Add Impetus to the Revitalization of the Old Industrial Bases, *China Daily*, September 2, 2013, p. 2.

4 Xi Jinping's Speech at the Conference for the 95th Anniversary of the Founding of the Communist Party of China (July 1, 2016), *People's Daily*, July 2, 2016, p. 2.

Communist Party of China insists that all is for the people and all depends on the people and that the foundation of the society building and social governance in China lies in the people and the power of the society building and social governance in China lies in the people too. Therefore, Xi Jinping said: "I would like to give the thumbs-up to our great people."[5]

If the society building and social governance in China is to persist in staying true to the original aspiration and continue to move forward, we must adhere to the concept of shared development.

As Xi Jinping emphasized: "To share the fruits of reform and development among the masses of the people widely is the essential requirement of socialism and an important manifestation of our party's commitment to serving the people wholeheartedly. The development we pursue is for the benefit of the people. The prosperity we seek is the common prosperity of all the people. The ultimate criterion of judging whether the reform is successful or not is whether the reform and development achievements are accessible to our people and are shared by the people."[6] A history of the society building and social governance in China is a history in which the Chinese Communists have close ties with the people, continuously increase the people's welfare and promote the people to share the fruits of development. Xi Jinping emphasized: "We should listen to people's voice anytime and be always ready to respond to people's expectations so as to ensure people's rights for equal participation and that enjoy equal development and work hard to safeguard social fairness and justice. We should make new progress so as to ensure that every kid is in school, everyone has work to do and get paid, every sick receives medical treatment and the elderly are taken good care of so as to safeguard and develop the fundamental interests of the overwhelming majority of the people, to allow more benefits from development to be more equally shared by all the people and to enable the whole people to advance steadily on the basis of economic and social development towards the goal of prosperity for all."[7]

---

5   Xi Jinping's 2015 New Year Message, *People's Daily*, Jan 1, 2015, p. 1.
6   The CPC Central Committee Organizes a Symposium of Non-Party People, *People's Daily*, Oct 31, 2015, p. 1.
7   The Party Literature Research Office of the CPC Central Committee, *Selected Important Literature After the 18th CPC National Congress*. Vol. 1, Central Party Literature Press, 2014, p. 236.

Adhering to socialism with Chinese characteristics in the new era and strengthening the society building and social governance in China, The Chinese Communists uphold the concept of "putting the people at the center", stay true to their original aspiration, 'bring peace to the world and stability to the country' to help the world and the country and benefit the people universally. As Xi Jinping pointed out in his report to the 19th CPC National Congress: "Everyone in the Party must keep firmly in mind that the nature of a political party and of a government is determined by those whom they serve. To lead the people to a better life is our Party's abiding goal. We must put the people's interests above all else, see that the gains of reform and development benefit all our people in a fair way, and strive to achieve shared prosperity for everyone." Advancing the society building and social governance in China, the Communist Party of China is ensuring and improving people's wellbeing and extending the benefits of economic developments to all the people more broadly and fairly so as to ultimately achieve the goal of common prosperity for all the Chinese people.